Call the Chaplain

*Spiritual and pastoral caregiving
in hospitals*

Kate McClelland

To John
with love aa best
wishes
    Kate
      x .

CANTERBURY
PRESS
Norwich

© Kate McClelland 2014

First published in 2014 by the Canterbury Press Norwich
Editorial office
3rd Floor, Invicta House,
108–114 Golden Lane,
London EC1Y 0TG

Canterbury Press is an imprint of Hymns Ancient & Modern Ltd
(a registered charity)
13A Hellesdon Park Road, Norwich,
Norfolk NR6 5DR, UK

www.canterburypress.co.uk

British Library Cataloguing in Publication data

A catalogue record for this book is available
from the British Library

ISBN 978 1 84825 636 1

Typeset by Regent Typesetting
Printed and bound in Great Britain by
CPI Group (UK) Ltd, Croydon

For Pat,
my rock

Acknowledgements

Dr Nicky Rudd – for inspiring me to be the best healthcare practitioner that I could be, instilling in me her values and dedication, making sure that all patients have the best holistic care possible at end of life.

Jill Hardman-Smith – for educating me on best practice at end of life, for opening doors for me where religious apathy existed and giving me a rounded understanding of spirituality in a clinical context as well as being a good friend.

Reverend Caroline Roe – for being a loyal friend and excellent colleague. For the personal sacrifices she made for me, always believing in my ability and calling.

Christine Smith – for her faith, determination and encouragement when recognizing something in me I had failed to recognize in myself.

Margaret Dillow (Mum) – for introducing me to the faith, and teaching me to search for my own answers to the questions of life.

Reverend Pat Nimmo – for giving me everything I needed, when it was needed.

Contents

Foreword

As the Head of the Hospital Palliative Care Team, I was lucky to have Kate assigned as the chaplain to the team. She attended our team meetings for nearly three years, bringing a unique view to the management of the distressed patient or relative.

Kate has written a book that demystifies many of the aspects of hospital life. She gives a very individual view and shows how to be a true advocate for the person in front of her. The book is a practical guide for anyone who works with people and an insight into the breadth of experience that she has built up over her years in the ministry. Each chapter has a subject that is well illustrated and concluded with a wise set of key points. She has covered topics that range from complex family relationships, through the challenge of mental-health problems to the importance of rituals. The book concludes with a chapter on sustaining oneself in the face of suffering.

The themes that shine through all these diverse topics are those of communication and the ability to concentrate on the needs of the person in front of you, thereby allowing them to express themselves in an effective way. The lack of judgement and acceptance of that person and their belief system, whatever it may be, is refreshing.

I can wholly recommend this book as a guide for anyone working in hospitals, both those in the chaplaincy team and anyone else who has contact with patients in whatever form.

Dr N. Rudd
Consultant and Head of Service for Palliative Medicine
Haematology & Cancer Services
University Hospital of Leicester

Preface

Dear Friends,

I hope you enjoy reading my book. It is an honest and open account of my experiences as a healthcare chaplain. It records the highs and lows of what has been the most difficult, disturbing yet privileged and enriching part of my ministerial journey to date. I always say that I wasn't called into chaplaincy, it happened out of a practical desire to 'move home' to be closer to my dad, whom we knew to be slowly dying. As a fun-loving, musical, all-singing, dancing Methodist minister, the last thing on my mind was to minister to the dying, and subsequently to those who have the most challenging mental illness. There's not much singing and dancing in that, you might say – but God has a wonderful sense of humour and a way of taking us down the right path at the right time, even though we may want to argue or barter. So here I am. I hope you find what you are looking for in this book, but mostly I hope that it aids you on your personal journey of pastoral care. Christina Rossetti, in her poem 'In the bleak midwinter', asks: 'What can I give him, poor as I am?' The answer is, of course, 'My heart'. It really is as simple as that.

May the blessing of God be upon you and the peace of God live in your hearts.

Kate

Introduction

When a person becomes unwell and needs to enter a healthcare environment – a hospital, hospice or care home – they can cease to be an autonomous person. Choices that previously have been taken for granted – the freedom to go out, choose what and when they want to eat, what to wear and when to get undressed, what procedures happen – can be taken away, causing a loss of dignity, self-respect and disempowerment. Spiritual wellbeing is central to a person's autonomy and an integral part in the healing process. Journeying with someone through the darkest valleys of their lives is a challenging, difficult and sometimes overwhelming task, yet an incredibly enriching, privileged experience. This book shows a personal insight into this pastoral ministry, the highs, lows, challenges and skills needed to equip all those people who feel called to care in this environment.

Within healthcare circles I believe there is currently a gap between theory and practice with regard to spiritual and pastoral care. Hopefully this book will go some way to bridging that gap. I aim to address some of the complex issues surrounding pastoral visiting in a healthcare environment while providing some practical tips to improve the patient experience. With reference to personal narratives, I will explore the pastoral sensitivities surrounding patient encounters, as well as some of the practical aspects of the roles of chaplains, clergy, pastoral visitors and volunteers. I will draw on many years of experience of caring for people as they face the challenges of illness, diagnosis, old age, mental illness, death and bereavement. I will give an honest and sometimes emotional account of my work and professional practice as well as tips I have learnt along the way. This is not an academic book, rather a reflective look at pastoral and spiritual care in a healthcare environment plotted by my own spiritual and pastoral journey. I will also reflect theologically on actual practice that has been gained from working in acute hospitals, community hospitals, secure and medium secure environments.

The aim of this book is to provide a resource to equip people from all walks of life for pastoral ministry in a healthcare environment. At the end there is a section of liturgies for you to use on your journey with those in need of spiritual comfort. This book is both for those people who are experienced or professional pastoral visitors and for those who are just beginning to consider pastoral ministry. A first consideration when taking on this enormous responsibility for caring for others is to know who we are as individuals and what knowing ourselves can teach us about caring for others.

Knowing who we are

Who we are as individuals cannot and should not be separated from the acts that we do and the reasons we do them. If you are considering a 'call' to pastoral ministry then the first step is to have a long, hard look in the mirror and ask yourself: Who am I? Why am I called to pastoral ministry? What is my role to be? It is only when we answer those difficult questions about ourselves that we can truly begin in the process of caring for others. Understanding why we have gone into an encounter and what we hope to gain from it is key to having a successful outcome.

I, for example, am a clergy woman, a minister of religion and a chaplain, but there is so much more to me than that. I am someone's partner, a mother, a sister, friend, daughter, animal lover, musician, writer and social activist. I remember on the eve of my ordination, my then Chair of District, a man I had the utmost respect for, came to visit me and asked me how I was feeling. While I was stumbling with words of expression that seemed totally inadequate for the task that was before me, he simply said: 'Well, there's no going back; you can never be un-ordained.' In a self-consumed state I didn't really acknowledge what he'd said. Many times over the past years, however, it has returned to me. Yes, you can stand down your orders, resign if you will, but I made a commitment before God and vow to care for others and serve God for the rest of my life. Every person who takes that vow should take it very seriously or they let themselves and their God down. You can never be un-ordained – for the rest of my life I am 'called to care' in the service of my God. If you are ordained then you will also have experienced that momentous occasion of ordination when you submit yourself to life-long service to the care of God's people. Yet ordination is only one route to service. The call to every Christian is to walk alongside those in need, to hold out the hand of friendship to those who have fallen and to love those whom others cannot or will not love. This is a high calling on our lives, yet it comes with the greatest of rewards. These rewards are to be found in the richness and privileges of sharing experiences with those you encounter.

Calling and your personal theology are important elements to embrace and understand. Time and time again you will be required through this ministry to look inside yourself to your personal resources. You will be called to say the right thing at the right time, to face situations that are unimaginable and that are personally very costly to you. Your own theological stance will be challenged and your faith shaken and tested. Having a clear understanding of why you believe and what you believe about God is vital. My theology is incarnational. It is grounded in a simple, clear understanding that 'God is with us' in this moment and in this encounter. I am called to reach out and touch the lost, broken and lonely, as God's representative on earth, with as much love, compassion and understanding as my humanness can manage.

Holding in tension that calling and being a real living human being that gets fed up, is selfish, can be unreasonable (apparently!) challenges me. It should not be underestimated but embraced. 'How do you do it?' Well, I do not try to be superwoman. There's a good reason for this. It does not work, people see through you. Be yourself, but know who you are. It never ceases to amaze me that God did indeed choose me for service, with all my faults and all my talents. But God also chose me to be all the other things I am and gave me a tool box full of interesting things to help me with the roles and responsibilities I have to face. In short, take it easy on yourself. Just do the best you can with the resources you have available on that day, in that moment. Don't waste negative energy wishing you'd done more or been better. Save your energy for your next encounter. It is a far greater use of your skills.

Knowing who you are at the moment of any encounter is a vital requirement for good pastoral visits. My best friend, who is also a clergy woman, recently was getting ready to visit her mum in hospital. This particular hospital stay, as for many families, had been fraught with miscommunication and frustration. As she put on her coat I noticed the clerical shirt peeping out and asked why she was wearing it. Her reply was, 'I will get in past the staff (out of visiting hours) and perhaps they will treat me better.' I know what she meant, of course. With the collar comes a certain authority, although not as much as it used to. In her frustration she was hoping to pull some sort of rank on the staff and get treated with more respect. She was hoping that it would lead to more information about what was happening to her mother and therefore relieve some of the family tension that was building. What she failed to realize was that, by putting on her collar, she ceased to be seen as her mum's daughter but rather her mother's spiritual guide (which she was not). It affected the relationship with her mother and the staff. It did not allow her to say the things she wanted to and she had to suppress her emotions. These were emotions that a daughter with a mother who was being ignored on the ward was entitled to feel, but which were not expected from a clergy person. Rather than treating her better the staff treated her with a coolness and detachment that comes when dealing with professionals on a daily basis. The collar became a barrier to a good pastoral visit in this case.

Nursing staff are not monsters, they are people like you and me. They are often overstretched and undervalued but they too have mothers, sisters, brothers and friends. I feel confident that had my friend rung the ward and asked politely to come at a different time for visiting with a reasonable explanation, they would have accommodated her. As a daughter, there would have been a level of understanding at what was happening to her mother and the frustrations that she expressed. There would have been a freedom to express those emotions without feeling she had let her vocation down. We are human beings with human emotions. We have a right to feel angry, upset, horrified, outraged when someone we love is being treated unfairly or badly, or even being abused. In theological terms it's righteous anger. On the back of righteous anger comes the turning of the tables, as Jesus did in the Temple with the money-changers and sellers of wares. When we are pushed to the limit and express ourselves correctly and coherently we can change things and make things happen for the better. However, we cannot take on every fight, for every person. We need to know when the time is right to turn tables and when is the time to be peaceful and bring comfort. Knowing who you are when you enter into your pastoral encounter will enable you to respond to the situation authentically.

So are you going into your pastoral encounter as a lover, daughter, mother or father? Are you pastorally visiting a friend, a colleague or a family member? Are you visiting in a professional capacity – clergy, chaplain or volunteer – or is it a personal visit? When we know who we are and what we are doing, we can respond to the encounter in the appropriate manner. It also allows the professionals caring for your loved ones to respond to us as we are, in all our weakness and all our imperfections. When I go onto the wards in my capacity as chaplain I am greeted by the staff in several ways. Some treat me with suspicion, as there is often negativity surrounding religion for many different reasons. Others, perhaps people of faith themselves or who have experienced chaplaincy before, will be respectful, and grateful for the visit to the ward. Often staff will make referrals for patients, some of whom have expressed a desire to attend a service of worship or have communion brought to the ward. Other referrals come because the patient is distressed, lonely or doesn't have any family to visit them. When I enter into a situation like this, I am the chaplain. I am not a daughter or friend. I have only one task to perform and that is to alleviate spiritual pain in whatever way I can. The encounter is not about me. My whole focus is to learn about the patient, to engage in their world and to help with their situation in any way possible. When I visited my dad in hospital, I did not want to be seen as anything other than his daughter. I wanted to ask the staff a whole range of different questions than those I ask as a chaplain. I wanted to make a fuss when he needed a drink because he would never want to bother anyone when they were so busy. I wanted to read his drug chart and ask why they had changed his medication. I wanted to weep, and I did, when I looked in the notes and saw they had recorded he had cried out my name in the night, and I did not want to apologize for those tears. We do not have to pretend to be someone we are not, we just have to be ourselves. Who we are is good enough for God; it should be good enough for us. We are human not divine.

So our ministry begins with our seeking to understand who we are; once we have that understanding, we are ready to look at the expectations of a pastoral encounter.

I

Expectations of a pastoral encounter

Introduction

Having established who you are and why you're visiting someone, you are ready to understand what makes a good pastoral
visit. This chapter considers three models of pastoral visitors:
the family member, the friend and the professional visitor.
Most of the skills are interchangeable and some are specific to
the role that you are embracing. It explores the practical skills
of good pastoral visiting, the understanding of spiritual care,
caring for others and knowledge of other faith traditions. The
purpose of the chapter is to show how to make a good pastoral
encounter into an excellent one.

What makes a good visit

It was on my first day as a chaplain, in an acute hospital trust
visiting my first ever patient, that I learnt the hard way that
good preparation is everything to a successful visit. I went
to visit a lady who had had an amputation. She was already
wheelchair-bound and paralysed from the waist down. She had
thought that her leg had looked infected and had been treated
in the community by the district-nurse team who had insisted
it was all right. It was when she was out shopping that members of the public had made comments about the smell of her
leg, and a group of young men had made cruel jokes at her
expense. This had obviously been a distressing experience for
her and she desperately needed to tell someone about it. Her

need of me was not of a practical nature, but to sit, listen and empathize. As she was a long-term patient, she had accumulated many possessions in her room and the one chair normally available to visitors was filled with a cacophony of equipment. The room was very hot, as it usually is in a hospital, and the window was not open. The smell from the catheter bag and wound was incredibly potent. I set the scene because if you are intent on hospital visiting, this is exactly the kind of situation you are likely to encounter. Aware of how upset she'd been at the young men's cruel jibes, it was vital that I made no reference at all to the smell by asking to open a window, and that my face did not betray any feeling of disgust, even when she insisted on showing me her wound.

Now unfortunately my family has a trait of being unable to listen to gruesome or detailed medical information without passing out. I know – why chaplaincy? Why me? God, I guess, and God's sense of humour! Most of us in my family have it apart from my son, who is a nurse, and my niece, who is a physiotherapist. The rest of us only have to hear the soundtrack of *Casualty* and we're gone, completely passed out! So needless to say, on this fateful day, after listening empathically to the entire saga, looking with forced interest at the amputation area, with all the surrounding smells, I passed out. To my credit, I did somehow manage to pray with the patient and get out of the room before I slid down the wall in the middle of the busy ward!

Needless to say I learnt a great many things from that encounter. Here are some tips to help make your encounter a positive experience for both you and the person you are visiting.

Identify yourself

When entering a patient environment the first thing you should do is identify yourself. Hospital, care homes and hospices are sometimes confusing environments. Patients are at different levels of recovery. Do not presume that they will recognize you, even if you are visiting a family member. Therefore it is wise to state clearly who you are when approaching the patient. This can be as simple as 'Hello, Mum, it's me, Maureen' to the more formal 'Hello, Mrs Smith, my name is Kate. I am the hospital chaplain. I have come to see how you are today.' This will help put the patient at ease and relieve any anxiety that may have built up within them. One of the main fears found in older people is that they are 'going mad', or getting dementia. Often something as simple as a urine infection can create confusion in patients, which may only be temporary but may mean that they do not recognize someone familiar. Some people can get into such a state of anxiety that it temporarily blocks out any rational thoughts. There have been many occasions when, after identifying myself, a patient has asked me if they are dying. Just seeing me and the collar can bring on thoughts that we may not have anticipated. Also I often get mistaken for either a social worker or a nurse, if I am wearing a blue clerical shirt rather than a black one. Again I learnt the hard way. On one occasion early on I entered a room expecting the patient to know who I was from my collar. She greeted me warmly as if she knew who I was, but clearly did not. I went to pull up a chair and when I turned round she had taken her nightdress completely off and was standing naked in front of me. She thought I wanted to examine her. I was shocked and embarrassed, but more importantly, she was mortified. No one wants the vicar to see them naked; it's an unspoken taboo. Starting your visit with clear introductions, including an explanation of why you are there, gets the visit off on the right foot and enables a more engaging and worthwhile encounter.

Gain consent for the visit

Do not presume that the person you are visiting wants to be visited. The autonomy of a person is often stripped away in institutions. They may have had a terrible night's sleep, had procedures before your arrival and had a stream of interruptions that has left them tired or irritable and upset. After identifying yourself, ask if it is convenient to visit and if they actually want you to stay. Remember that there is often very little choice available to them at this time. You are offering a vital and important service by giving them that choice. Be prepared for them to ask you to go away. It won't be personal! Chaplains, like other professionals dealing with often tragic and emotionally stressful situations, find they need a weird sense of humour! I had not been in the post long when my initiation came in the form of a meeting with Mr X. My colleague had suggested that he might like a visit from me. Perhaps, he said, he might like communion. I dutifully prepared my things and trotted off full of righteousness. As I approached the bed, Mr X smiled. 'Oh,' he said, 'you're a new one.' 'I wondered if you'd like me to give you communion today,' I said very seriously. 'Did you, dear?' he said and followed it with, 'No, I wouldn't. Now ∗∗∗∗ off!' Interestingly, the following Sunday he attended the chapel and was completely different! You never can tell. Nor should you presume that people will be pleased to see you.

Fetch a chair

If you are invited to stay, before anything else, fetch a chair to sit on. Never sit on a bed. This increases the chance of cross-infection to the patient. It's not good practice to start a conversation that might get deep or emotional then for you to break the momentum and have to say, 'Oh, hold that thought, I just need to go and find a chair,' or worse. Get it at the start. If it turns out to be a short visit it doesn't matter. If you are sitting down it has two effects. The first is that it looks to the patient that you are actually interested in engaging with them, at their level. Most professionals stand and speak down to them, often briskly while they are doing a procedure to them or filling in a form. This gives the impression that they are too busy to engage with the patient or that they are only half listening. When you draw up a chair you are saying, 'You are important to me. I want to listen to what you have to say. I have time to be with you.' Also, if like me you are of a sensitive nature, it's easier not to faint if you are sitting down with your feet firmly planted on the floor.

Be practical

Horrifying news stories of patients waiting on trolleys and dying of starvation and dehydration will not have passed you by. Such incidents are rare, but the reality is that often in a healthcare environment the staff are overstretched and things get missed. Many times when I visit a patient, their biggest concern is that they need the toilet and have been pressing their buzzer for a long time. One practical thing you can do in that situation is go to fetch a member of staff, or you may be able to assist someone to the toilet. There can be little more dehumanizing than needing the basic facilities and not being able to go. The same applies to food and drinks. On arrival, and before leaving, check if there is anything that is needed. Pour a drink; help them to drink it. Feed them if necessary.

I remember one incident where I had a referral from my own church. He was a lovely man in his nineties who had been a stalwart of the church, a local preacher and Sunday school leader, whom I had always respected and admired. I will never forget him weeping when I held his hand and told him who I was. It was pitiful. He had had numerous hospital admissions, usually in the middle of the night, from the care home where he lived. Young, inexperienced staff panicked in the night when his breathing became shallow. He sometimes had to wait hours in corridors while a bed was found, only to be discharged a few days later. His family had all died and there was no one to speak up for him. He had all but lost his sight and he told me that he had not eaten or had anything to drink because no one had fed him and he could not see to feed himself. The tray arrived and was taken away again because he could not see where the food was. He was too proud to ask for help and did not want to bother the staff. I spoke to them and was reassured that he would be helped. I did not have much confidence in that, so every day I timed my visit to coincide with lunch. Most wards have 'protected mealtimes' where they ask family and staff not to visit to ensure that all the patients have a proper chance of eating peacefully. If you identify to the staff that you would like to aid your loved one/friend to eat, this can usually be negotiated. I fed this gentleman while we chatted about the old days. It was such a humbling experience. We shared so much over food in those last days. It reminded me of Jesus, who always seemed to be eating with someone or other. I realized that the sharing of food allowed for a levelling of identities while meeting a basic human need. In the sharing of bread there was a sharing of stories, lives and experiences. My gentleman talked of John's Gospel and how it had guided his life. We talked about death and his desire to be left alone to die, his desire to be reunited with his wife and son and his faith which had upheld him through the trials of life. From those conversations I was able to explain to the care home where he lived and explained that he was in fact ready to die and asked them to stop calling for an ambulance every time they thought he was nearing the end. He just wanted to die at home, in peace, not being left on a trolley or resuscitated in A&E. They respected his wishes and that was the last time he was admitted. He died a week later peacefully at the care home which had been his home for the past 15 years.

Care of others

When visiting a patient, family member or friend, be aware of your surroundings. When we visited my dad in the care home we noticed that, as in a lot of care homes, many of the residents sat in the community lounge. One of the care assistants would bring in two large jugs of juice and some tumblers and then leave the room again to attend to someone in need. Many of the residents, including my dad, were not actually able to walk or pour themselves a drink. When you help one person and get them a drink, check the other residents and patients in the room. Not every client gets regular visitors, so be as generous as you are able with your attention. Be aware of your environment. The same can be said when visiting and saying prayers or giving bedside communion. Often there can be other people, perhaps not identified as religious or from other faith backgrounds, that are keen to join in with what you are doing. If it is appropriate include others. It also helps patients and service-users to bond with each other. Once I was visiting a lady and taking her regular communion when another patient asked if she could join us. My lady was delighted and together we shared a very precious service. They were a great support to each other during their stay in hospital and afterwards they became firm friends.

Other faiths

Knowledge of other faiths is essential when pastoral visiting in a healthcare environment. If you are a professional pastoral visitor, you will inevitably find yourself visiting someone, either patient or resident or relative, who is from a different faith background from yourself. Understanding other religions is vital to understanding the other person. The six major world faiths are Christianity, Islam, Hinduism, Sikhism, Buddhism and Judaism. Rather than focus on the difference between religions, I prefer to focus on the similarities. Most religions worship one God. Most people of religion acknowledge some kind of worship which includes prayer. Most religions have festivals and times of celebration, and most people following a faith are respectful of other people's beliefs and practices. There is nothing to fear from other religions and other faith practices. There is nothing more moving for me than when our Sikh volunteers at the hospital ask if they may join in our prayers. They are very respectful; it is not a requirement of the Sikh faith to attend regular prayer times (Sikhs can pray individually when it is appropriate to do so, unlike Islam, for example, in which Muslims follow set prayer times). I have learnt a great deal about other faiths and practices from my colleagues over the years and have enjoyed sharing my Christian faith with them. There is an infusion of Spirit when we share our traditions with our brothers and sisters. When we explain to someone outside our own tradition why we do something, we remind ourselves of its importance to us.

I remember explaining to our Hindu chaplain about Lent and it reawakening in me its importance and meaning, which sometimes gets lost among the familiarity of our traditions. We often sit together and he'll ask me questions about my faith and beliefs and I ask him about his. I think sometimes people are frightened of engaging with those of other faiths for fear they will try to convert them. This is not going to happen. The different faiths are rooted in their own history, traditions and cultures. When someone has a belief in God, there is no need for them to convert to another form of God worship, unless they desire to do so. There are plenty of people in the world that have yet to experience the love and knowledge of God without trying to convert people. So when you are visiting and are asked to pray for a person from another faith background, see this as a privilege. When I do so, which is often, I use God-centred language rather than Jesus-centred. I ask them what they would like me to pray for. I don't presume that I know what they want. You will often find that the shared humanity is enriching and humbling.

I had such an experience with a mother who had triplets, one of whom had died. I had taken the baby's funeral and, the following week, had called in on the other two neonates to check their progress and to catch up with their mum and dad, who were Hindu. Mum was really pleased to see me and we spoke at length about the baby she had lost. Her husband did not want to discuss the baby and seemed to want his wife to forget that she had had three children. According to Hindu belief the baby would be reincarnated into a better life, but the mum still thought her husband felt ashamed that the baby had died. Despite the difference in cultures and beliefs, we talked together about her baby and how much she missed him and how she felt to blame for his loss. That was just two women sharing in a story of loss and love a common humanity as a bond. At the end she asked me to pray for her and her baby. When I asked what she wanted me to pray for, the focus was on peace for herself and her husband, hope for the two remaining children and wisdom to handle the future. That I could do and I did. Who I was praying to almost seemed irrelevant; it was the verbal acknowledging of the need and another person's desire to share in her pain that was important in that encounter.

Spiritual care

When we are visiting someone in a healthcare environment, it is in the knowledge and understanding that we are providing spiritual care of the person. When we are inside a church, 'spiritual' is intrinsically linked with 'religious', but in a healthcare environment 'spiritual' means something that may or may not include religion. All people have the right to spiritual care. When someone is in an environment such as a hospital, hospice or care home, even if they do not have any religious affiliation, they have a right to spiritual care. In this case spiritual is defined as, in its broadest sense, the essence of a person, the thing that defines them, the thing that makes them who they are. This is more than a label, name or occupation but is entwined with their soul and belief system, even if that belief system is not religious. If you are a professional pastoral visitor or volunteer this may challenge you at your deepest level. The definitions can be vague. I think it is important to find a definition that you can align yourself to and work towards when you are participating in care in a secular environment. The one I use, and which is adopted by the Royal College of Nursing, is the definition produced by NHS Scotland. It is:

That care which recognises and responds to the need of the human spirit when faced with trauma, ill health or sadness and can include the need for meaning, for self-worth, to express oneself, for faith support perhaps for rites or prayer or sacrament, or simply a sensitive listener. Spiritual care begins with encouraging human contact in compassionate relationship, and moves into whatever direction need requires.

(NHS Scotland, 2009)

The key to providing spiritual care for the non-religious is for it to be patient/person-led. Use your listening skills for clues to where the distress is. For example, I was called to a patient that was deemed 'spiritually unwell'. She had no symptoms untreated, but she was listless, unsettled, disengaged and generally unhappy. The psychiatrists had been to see her but did not believe her to be depressed. When in doubt send for the chaplain! I spent a lot of time with this young girl who had had several bouts of Crohn's disease, a serious inflammation of the gut area. It was under control again but obviously for a young girl the indignities that Crohn's disease can bring were getting her down. She had had a stoma bag fitted and when she'd gone down into the canteen a member of the public had commented on her appearance, which had upset her. All around her room she had lovely pictures of herself and a dog. When I asked her about the dog her face lit up with delight. The dog, Bingo, was a very important part of her life and she was really sad that she couldn't see him during her stay. I went to see the surgeon and cleared a visit. I engaged in battle with the matron and got her blessing, and her mum duly brought Bingo into the hospital. It was just the thing to keep her going in the final weeks before going home and seemed to give her renewed strength and determination to get home again. A visit from her pet improved her spiritual wellbeing. Nothing religious in that encounter but definitely the dog's absence had affected her spirituality. Listening to what is important, trying to find a way to restore balance and meaning to someone's life, regardless of what or who gives that person meaning, is the key to spiritual care.

Conclusion

The best example of a good pastoral encounter can be found within the pages of the Gospels. Jesus was a good pastoral visitor and answered a 'call to care'. He went to many places where people sought him out to heal them and he sought to heal people. He healed many people in many different ways, not always physical healing but spiritual healing as well. First he listened to their troubles, sharing in their experiences, empathizing with their situations. He never judged but patiently listened to them and helped where he could. As with the haemorrhaging woman, he felt her touch the hem of his cloak and turned to her, looked into her face, saw the purity and hope within her soul and then healed her. He went to the house of Mary and Martha and shared food. He shared his experiences and they listened intently and learned from his wisdom. He came as friend, brother, teacher and ultimately king. On the occasion of the wedding in Cana, Jesus performed practical tasks such as sorting the wine out, almost working seamlessly in the background, so that the guests could enjoy the celebrations. He shared a moment with the Samaritan women at the well. This was a woman of different faith, different culture and different moral outlook, all of which would have normally been out of bounds to a Jewish man.

Time and again we see Jesus' desire to be there for people: his ability, even when he was tired and weary, to put other people's needs before his own. He reached out to those in need, sharing his love and kindness with all those he met. Jesus knew who he was, what his skills were, where he had the ability to help and also when it was not the time to change the course of destiny. He never sought the power that comes with fame and success. He was a loyal friend and wise spiritual guru. Jesus is an excellent model of a pastoral visitor that each and every one of us could and should aspire to be like.

In this chapter we have looked at what makes a good pastoral visit. We have covered the reasons for identifying yourself to the person you are visiting; gaining consent for the visit;

and the practical ways in which you can help your patient, others around you and yourself. We have looked at including others in our encounters; acknowledging the misconceptions of other faith traditions; and the difficulties of understanding and delivering spiritual care in a non-religious environment. We have drawn on familiar and perhaps unfamiliar theological texts to underpin our learning and to use in the future for support, encouragement, wisdom and guidance.

Key Points

- Identify yourself when you first approach the patient even if they are a family member. Do not presume they will recognize you.
- Gain consent for the visit – ask them if it is OK to stay. It is not personal if they say no.
- Fetch a chair before you begin your conversation. Do not sit on the bed.
- Be practical – check if they need food or water or help with the toilet. If you want to aid the patient to eat, always negotiate with the staff first.
- Remember those around you, other patients and residents, and include them where appropriate.
- Other faiths – if asked to pray, think about language; focus on God. Take the lead from the person requesting prayer. What do they want you to pray for?
- Spiritual care is for all people of faith and none. Identify a definition of spirituality that you can understand and work towards.

2

Understanding the person

Introduction

In this chapter we will look at how learning to understand the person can help to give more effective pastoral care. We begin by looking at what is meant by autonomy and identity, followed by how to give spiritual care to patients in light of understanding who they are as individuals. We will investigate how to help build relationships within the immediate family frameworks of our patients and service-users, critically assessing how and if our skills can encourage a real difference that has real meaning.

Autonomy

The concept of autonomy is found in moral, political and bioethical philosophy. In short it is the ability of a rational individual to make an informed, un-coerced choice or decision. There are few environments more incongruous than a hospital ward for allowing someone to exercise full autonomy over their life. There were posters in one of the hospitals where I worked that had a picture of an elderly lady with the words, 'I'm not love, or my dear, I'm doctor . . .' The purpose of the poster was to make staff aware that the terms of address they often use on the wards can be dehumanizing and strip away from patients their true identity. But it is not just people from an educated background that can lose a sense of identity and struggle with their autonomy on the ward. Small daily things for every patient, which we all take for granted, are stripped away in the confines of a busy hospital ward. They vary in degrees of impact and range. For example, not being able to make a cup of tea when you want it, or to have the food that you would like, or lack of options about religious observances or having to eat food that upsets you. Often people with food intolerances who have requested a different diet will find that their food has not made it to the ward or has been given to someone else along the way. Many times vegetarians find that the vegetarian option has run out and their only choice is either a jacket potato or a cheese sandwich. I am aware that some people will point out that you should be grateful that you have any food at all. Indeed, but we are not living in a third world country, and people in hospital are trying desperately to get strong enough to go home; food can become a huge barrier to recovery. Food has a big impact on religion as well. Often the multifaith chaplains work as mediators with the Trusts and on the wards to help those patients who for religious reasons cannot eat certain foods or who are trying to observe religious festivals and rituals, only to be stopped by the system.

A person's autonomy is not only affected by food. Every aspect of their stay in hospital impacts on their autonomy: when they can see their loved ones, when they get up in the morning, even when the lights are turned off at night. Then there are bigger choices and decisions that are also taken away from them. Sometimes they are told that there is no more treatment available to them or that they cannot have certain tests and investigations for whatever reason. Every time a choice and decision is taken away from them, it is taking away a small part of their identity, forcing them down a dark pathway that can cause spiritual pain. It is vital that we keep vigilant for those times and places when people's choices are denied them and support them, through that difficult process.

One such case was Susan. Susan had come in for a major surgery on an internal infection that would not heal. She was on a surgical ward and was struggling with recovery. Every time she got out of bed her wound would burst open and so she had lost confidence in moving around. The nursing staff had been instructed by the doctors to get her up and about. Over the weeks I got to know Susan, I found her to be a lady who was battling with a difficult and painful condition. She was not someone you would probably naturally warm to. I cannot quite put my finger on it but I felt she had a coldness about her. This, I hope, did not influence my treatment of her, but I think it did influence the other clinical staff attending to her. Susan did not suffer in silence. This came as no surprise to me, as her burden was great. Some people endear themselves to others, some do not. She did not. Determined to journey with her, I went to see her twice weekly for the duration of her stay in hospital. Each time I visited, I observed that she seemed to get more depressed. I think, owing to her demeanour, her depression was untreated and lost in the label of 'moaner'. I do not know when I first became suspicious that something else was wrong, something she did not want to tell me about. When one particular member of staff approached, Susan would become very withdrawn. I thought she might be being bullied. I started timing my visits at wash time. I waited until one particular member of staff took her for a wash, then crept up to the door and listened. I was right in thinking she was being verbally bullied behind closed doors, where it was thought no one could hear. A formal complaint was made and the member of staff removed from the ward.

Susan's case is a good example of where someone's identity was abused in a hospital environment, which had an impact on their autonomy. One of the most important aspects of the role of chaplain or volunteer is to be a patient advocate. It is vital that we keep vigilant, and make sure that we do not miss something important among the normal groans and grumbles of hospital existence. So, how do we provide spiritual care while respecting people's autonomy?

Spiritual care

A definition of spiritual care is given in the first chapter of the book, but how to give good spiritual care is slightly more complex. I have recently conducted fieldwork for my Masters in Palliative Care. My research explored nurses' perceptions of chaplains and their own provision of spiritual care at end of life. It was a constructivist grounded theory approach which, in layman's terms, means that I had no real idea of what the participants would say, but I would be led by the topics that they felt were important to them during the interview process. The results of the findings in the section on spirituality were quite interesting. First, the participants, 80 per cent of whom were from a non-faith background, saw spiritual care as religious care primarily. If the patient had no religious affiliation then nurses would look at spiritual care in the broader terms of essence, of what makes the patients individuals. Ninety per cent of the participants were not happy to have conversations with patients surrounding traditional faith topics; for example: Is there a God? Is there a heaven? If there is a God, why am I suffering when I have done nothing wrong and paedophiles go free? I found this interesting as the participants in the research were all specialist palliative care nurses and I assumed they would be having these conversations on a regular basis. Some were; others were not. The research also showed that the rarity of these conversations contributed to the nurses' reluctance to engage with patients at a level that could instigate these topics. Also in light of spiritual care being one of the four cornerstones of end-of-life care and given the same importance as physical, emotional and practical care, it did not seem to gain the same level of importance for many good, valid reasons.

If specialist palliative care nurses are not having the BIG conversations at end of life, it is even more important that as chaplains, clergy and pastoral visitors we arm ourselves with the appropriate responses for the BIG questions when and if they present themselves. These are the questions that could be asked of us, as people of faith, at end of life, by the frightened, lonely and lost. However, we require the ability to build a trusting relationship with patients before conversations of this nature can take place.

Relationship building

In an acute setting the emphasis is on discharge planning, and the speed of the turnover of patients can be quite alarming. There are some patients who make regular returns to hospital, especially on the oncology wards. The relationships that build up can be over years, with weekly visits or monthly visits. Also a bit like holiday friendships, even a short stay of a week or two in hospital can result in intensely intimate relationships being formed. It can be comforting for a patient with whom you have shared some very precious moments to see your familiar face appearing in the doorway following a repeat admission.

One of my favourite patients was Ethel. Ethel was given 18 months to live, but she was a woman with an inspirational sense of fight in her. She was determined not to waste a single moment of life or fun. Each time she came in for palliative treatment she would spend ages talking to me about where she'd been since our last encounter, and her plans for the next trip. One of her passions was cathedrals, so I got a book on all the cathedrals in Great Britain. When I saw her name on my list I would take the book along with me to her room, and even when she was really sick I would sit and read to her about the cathedrals she had yet to visit. She would lie in bed, needing to keep very still to stop the room spinning from all her medication.

I remember vividly the time I spent with her in the hardest of winters, with hail smashing on the windowpane and the failing light of a winter's afternoon bringing darkness ever closer. It was like the cancer itself, prowling round the perimeter fence of a compound, sniffing and searching for the weakness in the fence to tunnel through and devour its victim. It was then that I understood the incarnational context of John when he writes, 'The light shines in the darkness, and the darkness did not overcome it' (John 1.5), and I realized there in the darkness with my tiny flashlight, reading to a woman with such faith and strength, that the light will never be extinguished. I am not easily frightened, but I will be honest and say that those days frightened me. I would look out through the window and think, I am not strong enough to hold back the dark, how can I keep her, hold her, through this darkness. It was at those intense moments of loneliness that I would feel the presence of Christ beside me, gently touching my shoulder. Then the weight would be lifted, and my strength renewed. I remembered that it was not through my own strength that I was there, but through a strength sent by Christ with his promise to love and hold me in my own darkness. This was so that I may reach out and bring light to others.

Renewed, I would read to Ethel all the snippets of information in the book, from the history to what artefacts were within the great walls of the cathedrals she had yet to visit. If she was too poorly to take it in, when I went the next day she would ask me to repeat it all until she had taken in every morsel. Ethel would tell me about her last adventure and we would compare it with the information we had researched in the book. She sent me a postcard from all the places we had planned together in the small room with the rain battering against the window and the darkness prowling the perimeter.

Ethel's fight was an inspiration to me, as was her faith. She was determined to argue with God that it was not yet her time and I felt that I was part of her fight, her determination to live as long and as well as she could. Giving spiritual care to someone is complex. If they are a person of faith, they may want you to give bedside communion, to pray with or for them, to anoint them, to forgive them or to heal them. They may just want you to share in their pain, or their joys. They may want someone to ask those BIG questions. They may want a friend, a confidant, a spiritual guru or an advocate. They may just want you to see them, really see them just as they are and accept them at that moment with all their pain and their suffering. They may just want you to love them. Whatever you do or say, make sure that wherever you can, you try to make a difference.

Making a difference

I had the chance to make a difference with David and John. David was in the hospital on the oncology ward with lung cancer, but he was also HIV positive. He was terminally ill and the prognosis was that he only had a few weeks to live. The palliative-care team had asked me to visit this man, in his early 60s, who, although he had said he was not religious, was in what we term 'spiritual distress'. When I went to see David he seemed quite apprehensive when I walked into the room. This often happens on a first visit; the sight of the collar can be as much a barrier as a bridge. I used the skills in my tool box and chatted generally with him. I noticed a lovely picture of David and another man together and asked him if that was his partner. It was a risky strategy, but by doing so I showed my acceptance of his relationship. With such anti-homophobic propaganda surrounding religion, most gay people assume that the Church is going to be at best unsupportive, at worst discriminatory. Eventually I gained David's trust and he wanted me to come again and meet John at visiting time, which I did.

Over the weeks it came to light that David had become estranged from his family because he was living openly with John. David spoke to me of his parents, who were Christians, and the way in which they and the church community had estranged themselves from him. David and John had moved away and started a new life together, a life that had been personally fulfilling, yet blighted with episodes of discrimination. As David faced the end of his life, he desperately wanted to feel at peace about his life choices and wanted forgiveness from God. Together we explored his doubts, fears and some of the core texts that his parents and church had used to punish him all those years ago. We looked at the love David and John had shared, at the way they had supported and loved one another through lonely and difficult experiences, and they shared lovely memories of their 40 years of life and love with me.

It was a truly humbling experience. David realized before he died that he didn't need forgiveness, that what he thought was God's wrath was in fact the misuse of biblical texts by certain people to support their own prejudiced views. We held a service of blessing of David and John's life together where they both wept and said words to each other that they had never been able to say before. David was transferred to the local hospice where they were both treated with respect and dignity; most importantly, they were treated as any loving couple would be.

John was able to stay with David until he died. He died safe in the knowledge that God had not rejected him, that in fact he loved him and held him in the palm of his hand and would never leave him, and that one day he would be reunited with John again. I was privileged to be able to journey with them in the last few weeks of their life together. I was struck by their ability to be able to forgive those who had discriminated against them and to be an example of how to live and love in a relationship which can stand the test of time. My role was multifunctional. At times I was needed to be a listener, at times a spiritual guru, at times a practical organizer and at times God's fall guy. To bring spiritual relief to someone we may be called to take on multifunctioning roles: some situations completely unique, some that we can learn and improve on.

Challenging patients

Understanding who someone is as a person is only one aspect of ministry. Accepting them for who they are is a real challenge, especially when our natural instinct is not to like them. One such encounter was with Michael. When I was called to see him in the intensive care unit, he was desperately ill and not expected to live. The referral was for pastoral support for his wife, Sarah. She was the tiniest of ladies and really lovely. She was completely isolated; they had no family, and had not had children, and did not belong to a church community. I do not know if she was being physically abused, but it was quite clear that this man had bullied and verbally abused his wife. For several weeks Michael was unconscious, kept in a coma, and over that time I formed a relationship with Sarah. I thought her the most attractive woman; not physically, it was something about her gentleness, a small twinkle in her eye that I caught just occasionally and the way she laughed. She was seriously disabled and perhaps most people would have found her difficult or uncomfortable to look at, or they may have simply ignored her, but I did not. She had something about her. For several weeks we would chat in the relatives' room off the ward, before I went in to pray for Michael, and a bond was formed.

Eventually Michael woke up. I'm not sure if I am just being descriptive or simply unkind when I say he was just like Toad of Toad Hall. He was an ugly man. He was ugly inside and ugly outside. That's when the real challenge began. As Michael started to get better, he drained all the life and light out of his wife. She tended to his every need and he spoke to her in a degrading and humiliating way.

If you are looking for happy endings, I am afraid you may be disappointed. I wanted to walk away; I could not stand to watch it, I felt completely helpless. Of course I did what I could, making sure I spent time with Sarah away from the ward. I worked out what bus she arrived on and just 'happened' to be by the entrance to the hospital and so walked up to the ward with her when she came to visit. I tentatively talked to her about the options she had. The abuse was so entrenched, so part of who she was, that she was grateful that he had married her and honestly believed that he was a generous man for taking on a disabled wife. I felt I had no impact at all.

My relationship with Michael continued to challenge me. As chaplains we are called to attend to all without discrimination. After a few weeks Michael asked me to hear his confession. It is something that we do, but not very often. I sit behind the patient so that they are confessing to God not me. I can pray for forgiveness if they seek it; I cannot give it. Only God can give real forgiveness. Michael did not seek forgiveness; he wanted to tell me about several incidents that he had taken part in some years ago. They were not pleasant; in fact they were disturbing and sickening. I do not know if telling someone, God, enabled his healing; he certainly did recover physically and eventually went home, looked after by his wife.

During that time, I would often go and sit in the chapel after a visit. I found this the only way to cope with the situation. I would take all my feelings and emotions and pray them out to God, then leave them at the foot of the cross. It was too big for me to cope with alone. After these times of prayer I felt a sense of peace descend upon my body and then a renewed strength to go on to my next visit, without the burden of the previous one on my shoulders. A friend and colleague offered to share the burden and do some of the visits instead of me, but I felt it was something I needed to do, to face alone. To be professional in that situation was really hard and a most complex challenge to my ministry. I knew that I could not help or fix the situation, and I also knew exactly what Sarah was going home to. I felt so helpless and inadequate. I was angry with God. I found myself asking the same questions of God that people ask of me. Why let him live? But alas it does not work like that, and seeking the answers to human questions of that kind will never bring any real satisfaction.

The thing I learnt from that encounter is that people's identity is complex and sometimes underpinned or entwined with negativity and pain which are as much who we are as the positive loving bits. We cannot change who people are, nor should we try; we are only in control of our own destiny, not each other's. We can show people another path. We cannot push them down it, only offer to accompany them should they want to go down it themselves. I so desperately wanted to rescue Sarah, to bring about a happy ending, but sometimes there just is no happy ending. It may be that we cannot see the happy ending that has been written; we just take part in the story, like players on a stage. We only see a snapshot. We have to play our part, with dignity and integrity, and trust and believe that God has his hand upon all those people and places that we can't see, change or influence.

Sarah still writes to me, every three months. It is a beautiful letter, written in careful italic script, the like of which reminds me of a past age and time long gone. She writes to thank me for seeing her and to tell me that she thinks of me often.

Conclusion

We are called as people who care, to care for all people. It can be challenging to us when we do not like or approve of those people. It reminds me of the good Samaritan, a text I have heard interpreted so many times over the years. Preachers often encourage us to think of 'who is the other', who is the most likely person that you would want to ignore, to gain the impact of the story. For me the reality of the good Samaritan is not in thinking about it but just doing it. If you think about the negative aspects of the person you are called to minister to, or think about what they might have done, it will be reflected in your ministry. I battle every day with the challenge of judging others and it is my prayer that I can minister without this burden. Some things are mind-blowing, so do not think about them. Just concentrate on how you can minister to the person with integrity, love and compassion. Leave the judgement to God.

In this chapter we have looked at what it means to be an autonomous person in a hospital environment and how that impacts on a person's identity. We have explored not what spiritual care is, but how to give spiritual care in a clinical environment. We have looked at how we can build relationships with patients and relatives, even in the most difficult situations. We have looked at the importance of relationship-building and at ways in which we maintain integrity and professionalism when there is no happy ending.

Key Points

- Patients' autonomy and identity are challenged in a healthcare environment – help to give them as many choices as you can through mediation, practical help and pastoral support.

- Spiritual care is more than religious care. If a patient presents as non-religious, explore what gives them meaning in their lives – get to know them as individuals. Do not presume if they are religious that all their spiritual needs are also religious needs.

- Relationship-building – build relationships through whatever means are available to you. Find common ground that can be built upon, especially for repeated visits.

- Making a difference – working as an advocate, fighting discrimination and making sure the patient has their rights is a vital part of ministry and can really make a difference to the patient experience.

- Challenging patients – you won't like or approve of all the patients in your care. As a professional you are called to deliver the same care and compassion to all those in need. Find practical ways for your own support and wellbeing through these challenging circumstances.

3

Complexities of family relationships that serious illness highlights

Introduction

This chapter looks at the complexities of family relationships that are highlighted by serious illness. It assesses the challenges that pastoral visitors and those called to care face when they are supporting someone who has received bad news. It will look at the honesty needed in a relationship when you are asked a question the answer to which you know will be delivering bad news. There will be the identification of skills to help you as an advocate when families are at war or simply cannot cope. It will look at different sorts of behaviour and ways to support someone who is finding the pain of suffering much too difficult to bear. Finally, we will identify the difference between anger that is personal in contrast to anger directed at you because you are God's fall guy.

Breaking bad news

As a pastoral visitor there may not be many occasions when you are required to break bad news; that is usually the role of the doctor. I would like to say that they are well trained and do this duty well. Like many professionals that have multifaceted roles, they need to be good at their job – a brilliant surgeon or oncologist, for example – as well as an efficient communicator. Some are, and I know some excellent examples. It is usually when they are not good communicators, however, that the role of chaplain can be brought into the spotlight with regard to breaking bad news.

To begin, I think it's important to realize why communication sometimes breaks down. First, you have to remember that a doctor's whole psyche is dedicated to healing people and making them better. I have worked as part of a multi-disciplinary palliative care team. This team is focused on, among other things such as pain relief and symptom management, making sure that palliative patients are comfortable and those who have long-term non-curative illnesses who are going to die do so well. The team in the Trust where I worked were brilliant. They were talented, dedicated professionals, led by a consultant who was inspirational to me and valued the input that I was able to give to patients at end of life regarding spiritual care.

For patients to die well, we hope that they are without pain and that their symptoms are under control. We hope that they are peaceful, that they have dignity and all their wishes are met. The chaplain's role is for their spiritual care. The very fact that there is a specialist palliative care team shows that dying is not part of the normal everyday skills associated with medical staff in a hospital. Normally people come into hospital, get better and go home. It is very difficult for all the staff when they have to tell a patient that nothing more can be done to help them. No one wants that, and when bad news is given it not only ricochets through the patient and family, it also deeply affects all the staff. Doctors and nurses want to make people better; like us, they want a happy ending. Yet, sometimes there just cannot be an ending that is happy.

How we break bad news is not a textbook affair. There are many different ways in which we can either deliver bad news, or be part of the support mechanisms when someone is receiving bad news. How we comfort someone at the moment they need us can have an enormous effect on how they cope in the coming weeks and months. It is a huge responsibility. Never take it lightly.

There are many examples of supporting patients and families when they receive bad news but one I'd like to share with you was a little bit different in that it involved the role of 'touch' as comfort. I had one patient, Helen, whom I had been visiting. Her prognosis was good and she needed a bone marrow transplant. She had been regularly attending the chapel for some weeks. She was quite a surly woman, and her face gave away little emotion. She was probably somewhere in her late 50s. To be honest I did not really think she liked me very much. I went to see her on the ward and she was always quite short with me; I did not think I was being much help to her. Each time I visited her on the ward I asked her if she would like me to come back again and she would always say with a shrug, 'If you want to'. She never gave me any eye contact.

One day I went to visit her and her son was there. He told me she did not approve of women ministers and had had a falling out with her last one at the church, which went some way to explain her reaction to me. I persevered with her and eventually I felt a relationship was forming through a shared love of music and knitting – of all things.

One day I received a phone call from the ward asking for my attendance. Helen had asked for me to be with her, as the consultant has requested a meeting. She had not wanted her husband or children to be present but she had asked for me. We sat in the room together, the consultant explained everything thoroughly and sensitively, but the news was bad. Helen's leukaemia had progressed and they could no longer perform the bone marrow transplant. She was going to die. I will never forget the shock I felt. Everything had been going so well. She did not even look particularly poorly. The consultant left us alone in the room and she turned to me, looked directly into my eyes for the first time, and asked me to hold her. I can't remember how long we sat together. I just held her; she lay in my arms on the small settee in the tiny room off the ward, her head on my breast. I stroked her arm and kissed the top of her head. I did not tell her it would be all right, because it was never going to be all right ever again. All I had to give to this surly, cold woman, who could not show her emotions, was my physical touch, and I gave it to her willingly.

Eventually when she was ready we got up and walked back to the ward. Helen was a shadow of the woman she had been an hour earlier. She would not let me leave her and did not let go of my hand until her family came in that night. She asked me to relay what the consultant had told her. I had to break the bad news to the family. I saw this as a great responsibility and did it with as much empathy as I could.

The words I used were simple and factual, sensitive and gentle, but for me it was the power of touch that stayed with me from the encounter. I do not think she had been touched by anyone for such a long time, shutting out the world and the emotions that come with the risk of loving and being loved. I held her hand a lot in the following few days. We said very little – she was a woman of few words – but there was something in her letting me touch her that had broken through a barrier, and slowly a peace descended on her.

Her husband and grown-up children could not face being with her at the end. They were not a close family. Death is not always like in the movies, and they opted to stay away in the final hours. Helen did not speak about it; as I said, she was a woman of few words. In her final hours she asked me to read the Psalms to her – any that mentioned music – and to hold her hand. Breaking bad news is not just in the words we use. Being prepared to reach out to someone in whatever way they need you to, being as honest as you can, sensitive, caring and empathetic, all help to make receiving bad news a more bearable experience. It could possibly be life-changing for you as well. Every time I read the 'musical' Psalms I think of Helen, and I think I always will.

When families are at war or cannot cope

It is a well-documented fact that stress brings out the worst in people. Hospitals, care homes and hospices are all environments that are likely to bring out the worst in people, particularly family members and close friends of someone who is ill or possibly going to die. We all can identify with the concept of wanting to protect those we love, or make sure that they have the best treatment and care. Unfortunately what that actually means in reality is a somewhat grey area. It is at these moments that old family tensions, or even current family tensions, can come to the surface. There have been many occasions when I have called to see a patient to find family members already there. Usually, if this is a normal 'pastoral' visit, I introduce myself, identify the reason for my visit, make a quick assessment of what is going on in the room and leave. Some hospital wards are strict on visiting hours and a patient's moments with their family are precious, so I do not want to take vital time from their visits. However, do not just see that the family are there and 'not bother' going in. It's important that the whole family get support if they need it. Allowing them to see that you are around, that someone else is visiting Mum or Dad, often reassures them, and a contact has been made. I find that following such an encounter family members may come to the chaplaincy office and ask to speak to a member of staff regarding any concerns they have. Sometimes a distressed family will make us their first port of call on a hospital visit. We are often seen as separate from the nursing staff, with whom they may not have a good relationship. We can often work as mediators, sorting out any issues or concerns the family may have with the ward, and alleviating their stress.

Individuals or families who are at war with each other can be a challenging context and one that anyone can suddenly find themselves in the middle of without even realizing it. First, please remember that you are not a social worker, trained counsellor or Jeremy Kyle. You can only respond to the situation that you see before you with the facts that you have to hand. Remember that these family tensions have probably been around for many, many years. Often family will try to get you 'on their side' to see their point of view. I had experience of one such disastrous encounter where I was called to the ward to visit a patient, Luke, who was told he was dying. Luke's 'partner' was in attendance. She was a good 20 years his senior; she was very attentive, seemed to be very concerned for him, taking him to the toilet and fetching and carrying for him.

Luke was an alcoholic and his liver could take no more. The doctors had told him he had only hours left and that his family had been called in, as he had put them down as next of kin. His partner was very disturbed when she realized his family had been called; she told me how awful they were and gave a list of the terrible deeds that had been done to her. Within the hour, after sympathizing with her, which was my first mistake, the doors of the ward flew open and what can only be described as a herd of very large, formidable women burst through the doors and made their way down the ward. As I got up ready to introduce myself, one of his sisters flew at the partner with her nails out and I had to do a body block to stop her scratching her eyes out. I felt like Obi-Wan Kenobi fighting Darth Vader; she was vicious. Fortunately I had recently completed my advanced training course and I could recall all the things to calm and defuse a situation. Now for the reality: I nearly had my shoulder dislocated holding them apart and I got poked in the eye. There was no back-up from the staff, interestingly – they had completely disappeared. That was the first of many encounters with this family.

Now you could be forgiven for thinking they were a family that Jeremy Kyle would love on his show but in truth they were not. They were just like me. Luke was only a few years younger than me. We had been at the same high school. He was from a 'normal' loving family, but he had lost his way. He did not die, and he and I had some very deep, soul-searching conversations over the following months of recovery. The family tensions did not go away. The family blamed his partner for encouraging him to drink and buying the alcohol for him. His partner thought his family were cruel for wanting to stop him drinking and enjoying himself. I was never going to sort that one out and it was not my job to try.

When dealing with families in tension remember that you are not responsible for making everything all right. Your responsibility is making sure that the patient is as least distressed as possible. I remember with Luke's family one day asking them all to step outside and giving them a real telling off as they were arguing over his bed. It was not good for him. I did not get involved in the whys or wherefores, just the situation on the day. That was a daunting task. They were quite scary, but eventually I did earn their respect. You can only deal with the presenting issue. Do not take sides. Empathize but do not sympathize, and remember who you are in this. You are the pastoral visitor, not the social worker, doctor, counsellor or friend.

When pain is too much to bear

The previous section focused on family tensions surrounding hurt and anger. However, family tensions can manifest themselves in more gentle, emotive ways, and as chaplain, clergy or volunteer you may be asked for advice on certain situations. One really contentious issue that often raises its head is the DNR form: Do Not Resuscitate. I have been with many families who are beside themselves over this issue and it can divide the family. This is one issue, but there are many like it: whether to continue invasive treatment that has a low success rate; whether to operate on someone elderly who has suffered; whether to abort a baby with abnormalities. There are times when a hard decision needs to be taken, for example, when to switch off the life-support machine, or whether to withdraw active treatment. These decisions would shake even the strongest of families. You may have been involved with the family for some time, you may be seen simply as a person to be trusted or you may be called to be a mediator. You never know how these situations will affect individuals and families and when you may be suddenly part of the picture.

On one such occasion I was called to Kerrie and her husband Peter. She was 31 and her husband a similar age. They had desperately wanted a baby and had been through several rounds of in vitro fertilization (IVF) treatment. The final attempt had been successful, only to get to the 24-week scan to find out that the baby had brain abnormalities and was unlikely to survive for long after birth. The couple were distraught and a decision on termination was needed. They asked to see a chaplain and I was in attendance. The couple were from Christian families but neither had been attending a church recently. Kerrie was resigned to the fact that there was no hope for her baby and that an abortion was the only option. Peter, however, was being influenced by his parents who were practising Christians from an evangelical background. They were insisting that a miracle could happen and were engaging with members of their church in vigils of prayer for the baby to be healed, and had insinuated to Peter that they felt it would be wrong to listen to the doctors and should leave things in God's hands. Kerrie and Peter asked me what I thought they should do.

Much as in the previous section, the same rules apply. It is important on practical issues that you do not get tempted into giving medical advice. You are not the doctor, midwife or nurse. They will all have given their medical opinion. You should not add to that information. What I did was get them to talk to me about the baby, about the struggles that they had experienced. I asked them to tell me how they felt about it and what their thoughts were around aborting the baby. When they began to open up it was clear that they had been focusing on what other people had been saying and their advice, rather than listening to each other. Kerrie was able to admit her fatalistic attitude which was connected to the difficulties and disappointments around IVF. Peter was able to admit that he had been concerned with not letting his parents down but did not want to put himself or Kerrie through the pain of waiting, only to lose the baby all over again. They asked questions about heaven and hell, in their simplest forms, and I was able to reassure them of the love of God surrounding this baby. I gave them space to be angry at God and to ask the unanswerable questions without giving platitudes or slick answers that actually mean nothing in the real world with real situations. I then mediated with Peter's parents and explained how Kerrie and Peter felt as the procedure was completed. Instead of using their language of punishment and miracles, I talked to them of respecting difficult decisions and supporting Kerrie and Peter with love. I did not want to change their faith or their beliefs but I did want to change their attitude.

There are times in our adult lives when we have to make decisions that are hard and painful. Only *we* are responsible for those decisions. Truly loving someone is respecting that they have the right to make decisions for themselves and their families, even when we do not agree or cannot understand them. Kerrie and Peter popped into the office 18 months later and introduced me to Laya, a beautiful little girl with big brown eyes. They will never forget their baby boy, but it was not to be. Peter's parents dote on her and spoil her, like all grandparents should. We cannot see into the future or predict what lies ahead (thank goodness), we can only have faith in the moment.

God's fall guy

When I am wearing my collar I take my role very seriously. Normally a fun-loving girl with a wicked sense of humour, I see my role when I am wearing my collar as 'God's representative on earth'. As with all representatives, it is great while things are going right, joyous even, but pretty hairy when things go wrong. I sometimes think that God chose me for service because of my broad shoulders and thick rhino skin. When people and families are in a healthcare environment, they are often dissatisfied, feeling unwell, and afraid. All of these feelings can and do manifest themselves in anger. Enter stage right:

clergy with collar, or volunteer from the hospital or church. At that moment you are God's representative on earth and you may be in for a right rocket. There have been so many incidents of people being angry with God and taking it out on me that I hardly know which one to pick as an illustration.

I will share with you the story of Beth, the lady in the red dress. Beth was a complex, sweet-natured lady. She had just turned 59 when I first met her. It was a situation where her devoted husband, Jason, had come by the office wanting someone to talk to. I made him a cup of tea and he just needed to tell someone the news that the consultant had told him. His wife had cancer. Beth was still out cold from the procedure that she had come in for and Jason was to break the bad news to her when she woke. He told me how lovely she was. He had married her late in life. Her first husband had left her owing to her suffering from obsessive compulsive disorder (OCD). But Jason in a most simple way had said it was OK. They had found ways to cope with it. He had understood her at a deep level, and Jason had not tried to change her, to tell her not to be silly. He had listened to her anxieties about cleanliness and her need for certain washing rituals and had followed them. Together they had worked out the best way to keep Beth from getting anxious, which kept the OCD at a minimal level. I do not think I have witnessed such devotion in a couple before. They had wanted children but been unable to have them, and having lost two babies to miscarriage had contented themselves with being just the two of them. Jason was dreading telling Beth about the cancer because the procedures and the uncertainty of prognosis would make her anxious and that would make everything so much more intense.

I followed Beth's progress through the year. The doctors decided that operating was not viable and that palliative care was all that was left for her. I next came into contact with Jason when he was sitting in the church for a Sunday morning service. He had come to gain sustenance before visiting Beth. They were trying to get Beth strong enough to return home, where she wanted to die. After the service I went to chat to him and he said he had brought some photos to show me. Beth had wanted to leave something positive behind and a few months previously had been for a photo shoot wearing the most beautiful flowing red dress. The photographer had captured her perfectly: smiling, laughing, with her dress dancing like flames, flames from a fire that was still alight, still burning bright, a light that I knew then could never be extinguished by death. It would always live on in the hearts of those who loved her. She was a beautiful woman, loved at her very core. That kind of love lives for ever.

When I went to see Beth for the last time, she asked Jason to leave us for a few moments. She spoke of her anger at God, how she could not get over how he had let her down, how it was blocking her ability to be at peace. She wanted to shout and scream, 'Why me?' She was struggling to pray and felt that God had abandoned her. I suggested that she say it all to me. I gave her permission, if you like, as God's representative, to tell me. I reassured her that God had not abandoned her, but because she felt he had, to use me as mediator. I told her to say everything she needed to say to God, through me; to get mad with me. I put the 'do not disturb' sign on the door and sat quietly in front of her. I never broke eye contact with her and listened as all the negative fearful things she could not say to anyone else came out. Eventually she lay sobbing. I kissed her head and left the room, and she slept.

God is big enough to take our anger and our fears and doubts. If you are representing God, you too need to be big enough to take them without letting them into your own psyche. When I left Beth I went straight to the chapel and prayed for her and her soul. I left everything she had said at the foot of the cross. Then without burden I walked away to my next encounter.

Conclusion

It is not clear from the Gospels the extent of Jesus' family. What we do know is that he had a mother, a father and, probably, brothers. He certainly had people around him who loved him dearly, who did not really understand the full nature of his call, but loved him completely. Jesus understood the complexities of relationships, the petty rivalries of siblings, such as James and John, each wanting to be seen to be the most important to him, when they argued over who would sit on the left of him and who would sit on the right. He understood Judas's betrayal and loved him despite knowing what he would do. He understood the different sorts of love, such as the love he felt for John, his closest friend. We see Mary's love of her son, her sacrifice as Jesus chose to not defend himself against the cross, when he could have been saved, and she watched him being murdered. Mary must have known what it was like to be angry with God, but to still love him at the same time. Jesus in the upstairs room knew the importance of touch when Thomas reached into his open wounds and, in doing so, was changed, made new. Jesus knew the complexities of life and of the one rule not fitting all. There are many examples through the Gospels of Jesus finding different ways to show us how to live with one another. His greatest lesson was to teach us to love each other. Listening, touching and accepting are all part of loving one another in the complex relationships that we form in this life.

We have looked at the complexities of family relationships, how to remain focused on your objective and not get sidetracked into taking sides. We have looked at the skills needed when breaking bad news and the different ways in which we can support and comfort those who are facing bad news. We have looked at the role we can take when families have a difficult decision to take and not everyone agrees on the outcome. We have looked at the way in which we can play our part as God's representative when people need to express anger, and the skills needed to make sure we do not become emotionally challenged by other people's needs.

Key points

- When breaking bad news there are many ways in which facilitation can take place, including the use of touch.
- When families are struggling to cope introduce yourself, albeit it briefly, so that families know that you are there to support them as well as the patient.
- Do not take sides.
- You are not a social worker, doctor, nurse or counsellor.
- When pain is too much to bear, pick your language wisely; look behind obvious behaviour to what is really going on.
- If you have been given the authority of the collar, wear it with respect, dignity and compassion – it is a privilege and this is a servant ministry.
- Allowing someone to be angry at God through you can unblock barriers to inner peace – make sure you do not carry that pain with you; leave it at the foot of the cross.

4

Communicating in difficult circumstances

Introduction

In this chapter we will look at the skills associated with communicating with people in difficult circumstances. We will remind ourselves of the benefits of having good listening skills. We will look at how we can interpret a situation quickly and efficiently. The use of body language in a clinical environment will be assessed for its merits, and barriers and challenges that can stop effective communication will be identified. To begin we will look at the skill of listening.

Listening

It was many years ago that I did my first counselling course, long before I'd thought about pastoral ministry. I remember the course leader really clearly. She taught me two things. First, she would not begin the session until she had gone round the room and asked everyone to say one thing that was good about the day. You would not believe the amount of time that took, because so many people would say, 'I've got nothing good to tell.' Eventually as the weeks progressed we got round the room quicker and people would come prepared. It was at the end of the course that she told us the reason for her icebreaker. She wanted us to start the session off on a positive note not a negative one. By doing this it influenced how we approached the session and this impacted on what happened to us and how we behaved. To this day, as soon as I wake in the morning, I lie in bed until I can think of something good to be thankful for before I get up. It puts me in the right frame of mind for the day ahead. The second thing she taught me was to listen.

Listening comes easier to some people than to others. If you are like me and like to talk, you have to try harder and learn the techniques to make you into a good listener.

The art of listening is not rocket science yet so many people are not good at it. When was the last time you observed your own behaviour? Are you really a good listener? You may think you are but are you really?

What you have to remember here refers back to the introduction of the book and the identification of who you are. If you are a chaplain, clergy or volunteer you are not at the moment of contact in the role of friend. You are the professional pastoral visitor. What this means is that you are interested in what the patient has to say. The encounter is not about you and would not fall into the realms of a friendship; friends are interested equally in each other's lives, joys and sorrows. A pastoral encounter is very different. When we listen carefully we pick up cues as to what is important to the person and which way they want to take the conversation. We do not, or should not, steer the conversation in the way we want it to go, or make it about ourselves.

When I left my last church appointment after seven years they held a leaving party for me, and as part of it they decided to do a Kate Quiz. Twenty-one questions about 'Our Kate'. The table to score the highest was my family table and they only got seven. I saw this as a compliment (not the family bit, I despair at them! They were probably too busy talking!). If I have done my job properly people should not know a lot about my life, troubles and woes. That is for my family, friends and partner. My pastoral conversations are focused on the patient. They set the agenda; they decide what we discuss and how deep they want to go, not me. Of course, occasionally they will ask me a question, but the conversation should not be led by me, or be about me. To achieve this requires listening.

When I am conducting training sessions for pastoral visitors regarding listening, the first thing I get the group to do is break into pairs and tell their partner some bits of info about themselves. They tell their partner their name, where they live, why they decided to volunteer, for example. Then the other person feeds back and introduces their partner, retelling the information that they have just got from them via listening. It is amazing how many people get details wrong because a lot of them have not done the exercise before and they are thinking, 'What am I going to say?' Concentrating on what to say next blocks out their ability to listen to the other person. Rule one: relax, empty your mind and focus on the task at hand. Do not be thinking through what you're going to say next. Let it just come. I like to think of communication as a tool box full of useful things to help you with the job in hand. Here are some tools for your box to help you.

Reflection

One way to help yourself and to show the patient that you are listening to them is to use the tool of reflection. When a patient has said something, you reflect back what they have said. For example:

> Patient: I found that conversation with the stoma nurse really difficult.
> You: So you found the conversation with the stoma nurse really difficult?

It is a really helpful technique for the patient to hear back what they have said and reassures them that you are listening. It also buys you valuable thinking time if what they say to you is challenging.

Clarification

Clarification is another tool that is very helpful, especially if a patient is giving you a lot of information or speaking quickly because they are emotional. For example:

You: So what I think you are saying is that you found the news very difficult to take in because of the way the doctor spoke to you?

This shows that you are listening and gives the patient an opportunity to correct you if it's slightly wrong.

Summary

Summary is very helpful, particularly if you are in a mediator role. It allows for you, in your own words, to summarize what you think has been said. This is a useful tool if a lot is going on or there is more than one person speaking to you at once. It not only shows you have listened, it is also helpful in a more formal environment. So after a short period of speech, sum up in your own words what was said, for example:

Patient: I am really unhappy about the way in which the nurse spoke to me, I was only asking her because I didn't hear what the doctor said, she did not have to be rude.

You: I can see that you are upset by the way in which the nurse spoke to you. You did not manage to catch what the doctor said. (*You can then offer an observation and solution*)

You: It must be quite worrying for you. Shall I ask the doctor to go over the procedure again so that you feel more confident with it?

Interpreting situations

When you arrive at your patient, you need to interpret what the situation is. Even if you know the patient, you do not know if they have had an upset, been told difficult news or are simply not feeling well. So although we are now ready with our listening skills we need to make our assessment. When I enter a room, especially when I have been called out in the middle of the night to a patient who is dying, I find myself making a quick assessment of the family dynamics. Be ready to do this; you may only have seconds for it. A common situation is when the patient is religious but clearly the family are not. Sometimes you have to judge what is going on in a room and often this is when it is dimly lit. Interpreting body language is a real skill; common cues are lack of eye contact, shuffling of feet, arms crossed over the body; sometimes family will leave the room when I arrive. These are all signs that the family feel uncomfortable with my presence – not me personally, but what I represent, i.e. God. I have found that men especially find the emotion and difficult decisions surrounding death quite hard to cope with. At this point you have to read the signals and try to make some effective inroads. As always, introduce yourself and ask others in the room to identify themselves. It is helpful to know who you are talking to as there is usually a subconscious hierarchy in the room. Try to feel where the tensions are, and smooth the way as best you can. Never tell the family what you are going to do.

If the patient is unconscious ask the most senior member of the family and the person you deem to be the closest to the patient what they would like you to do. I had one situation where I was called to a patient nearing death and I walked into the room, introduced myself and prepared to say some prayers. Fortunately I asked the family if this is what they would like, only to be greeted by: 'Oh no, his own vicar came this afternoon. We wanted to ask if you know the price of a burial and if it's cheaper for a cremation.' This was not the most inappropriate conversation I have had over a death-bed but it comes up there as pretty close. Do not presume that you know what the family want from you, do not presume you can deliver all they want, and accept that you cannot make everyone happy.

Verbal interviewing skills

One of the ways we assess situations other than assessing body language is using verbal interviewing skills. Using the voice is the most common skill. We need to think about tone, pitch, clarity and volume. Using a sing-song 'Peggy Mount' voice may not be the most appropriate way to approach a patient who has just been told bad news. A calm tone, with a regular pitch, speaking nice and clearly, is the best start-off approach. I do not raise my voice unless the patient clearly cannot hear me. I do not know why, but older people tend to find it most annoying that everyone presumes that because they are older they cannot hear. It does not cost you anything to repeat the question, but if they are annoyed at you to start with it is harder to break down the barrier and build a relationship.

Questions

There are several questioning techniques that you can use, each with a different anticipated response. Bear in mind that you want the patient to determine the agenda for the discussion, so this should not be a round of questions, but you do need what I call a 'hook in' to get you started. Particularly if you are cold calling, it can be difficult to get a conversation going. The first type is the broad open question. The reason for using this is so that you are not influencing their thoughts. The question will normally start with 'how', 'what' or 'would' – How are you today? What did that feel like? Would you like to tell me about that? The downside to this type of questioning is that it is so broad it can be vague and the patient might be unclear what to say to you.

The second technique is the open directive question. This questioning style is still open, i.e. does not require a 'yes' or 'no' answer, but puts more of a focus on the conversation. For example: How did you feel when they told you the news about your treatment? Would you like to tell me about what is making you distressed?

The third questioning style is the directive question. This is used during a conversation to gain clarity on what has already been said. Use 'who', 'where' and 'when' but with a closed element. For example: Who said you could not go home today? Where is your preferred place to die? When would you like me to come and give you communion?

The fourth questioning style is the closed question, where there is no opportunity for a response other than 'yes' and 'no'. There are times when this style of questioning is appropriate but be aware that you are using it and why. A closed question means that there is no room for a freedom of expression from the patient and it can seem quite oppressive and leading.

One pitfall of using verbal interviewing skills is that it is too easy to ask leading questions. 'I expect you were frightened when you heard the news?' 'That is lovely, isn't it?' We all do it for good reasons, but try to avoid it. You are putting your perspective on their situation. Remember that a patient is a vulnerable adult and open to suggestion. If you use leading questions, it is unlikely they will be able to say how they actually feel. Another pitfall to avoid, especially when dealing with older people or patients with dementia or learning difficulties, is asking multiple questions. We start off with one question, then if they do not respond, or just do not respond quickly enough, we fire off another one. Remember that hospitals are strange disorientating environments. The rule is one question at a time.

Body language

Body language, both the assessment of others' body language and understanding how we come across, is also a useful tool. There are two things to take into consideration here. Body language assessment has been around for a long time and most people know the common traits. If I cross my arms then I am being defensive. If I sit forward in my chair I am anxious. If I sit back with open arms I am relaxed, and so on. So we have to take into account not only what our body language is saying but what other people will be interpreting from that behaviour. It is confusing. An example is that if I go onto a ward and I am cold sitting by the window, I might want to cross my arms over my chest in an involuntary action to keep warm. The patient, however, will probably see that movement as a sign of my being defensive or that I'm putting up a barrier, when I am actually cold. So body language has a twofold element. First, be aware what your body language is expressing, and then be aware what the patient might pick up from it. One patient had had a terrible infection that was taking weeks to heal. He had a drain that was taking the infected fluid into a bag next to me. I was sitting forward in my chair listening to him intently and he suddenly said, 'I'm so sorry about the smell, I cannot do anything about it.' I reassured him that it was not a problem at all, and he said, 'It was the way you were sitting; it looked like you could not stand the smell.' It *was* awful, and probably subconsciously I had betrayed my thoughts through my facial expression. Since then I always check my facial expressions and posture very carefully. He obviously felt really conscious about it. I did not want to add to his embarrassment but clearly had.

Barriers and challenges

There are lots of barriers and challenges to communicating that are covered in different parts of this book, but one area that I want to focus on is empathy NOT sympathy. I cannot express this point enough. It links into everything that I have said and it is the biggest barrier and challenge to us as pastoral visitors.

The difference is simple: empathy is *you* – sympathy is *I*. Of course it is more complex than that. When we have sympathy with someone we enter into their emotional space and *share* in their agony and pain. We walk alongside them carrying them on our backs, to try to ease their burden. Remember the poem 'Footprints in the Sand' with its imagery of Christ carrying us at the darkest moments in our lives: we thought we had been abandoned only to realize that we were being carried by him.

When we have empathy with someone we enter into their emotional space and *acknowledge* their agony and pain. We walk alongside them holding their hands, not carrying them on our backs, hoping it will ease their burden but also acknowledging that it may not. I love the footprints poem but we are not Christ. We cannot possibly carry that much pain on our shoulders without very quickly falling into the sand ourselves, unable to move from the weight upon us. When it is our family and friends we have sympathy, we carry them, love them and hold them. When we are professional visitors we empathize, and in doing so we are able at the end of the day to leave the pain and agony at the cross and go home to those we love. It may seem hard or clinical, and if you are beginning on your pastoral journey you may find that you disregard what I have said and plough headlong in. You will not be the first or the last. However, if you really feel called to pursue this ministry and you want to survive in it, take the warning seriously.

On a practical note, and to come full circle, sympathy usually ends up with *I* and that means bad communication skills. Many people come to the office asking to be volunteers because of the experience that they have had, which they feel they want to share with others. This happens particularly with people who believe they were 'healed'. Those volunteers never get past the starting block because you know they are going to go straight onto the ward and say, 'Well, yes, *I* had that, but *I* was fine.' Sympathy, not empathy. In fact if you are thinking of volunteering and have had an experience of a hospital stay I would suggest you volunteer to work in a completely different ward to help you not to make that mistake.

Reflecting back to my 'Kate Quiz', the patient should not really know anything about you. It is not about you but about them. Telling them that you were 'healed', and are now OK, or out of the woods, whatever language you want to use, is not usually very helpful to someone else facing their own very personal experience. Each case is unique. The worst thing is to normalize someone's experience. I remember one volunteer who visited on the oncology ward and only after several years of working together did she one day tell me that she had had cancer some years ago. I would never have known and as far as I know she never told any of the patients. She was a good example of an excellent volunteer visitor. She wanted to reach out to people, whom she could identify with as she had gone through the feelings and emotions that they were going through, but she made each encounter about them not her. Her spiritual connection was with the bond of suffering not with the sharing of her story.

Wounded healer

At theological college we learnt the different models of pastoral care, and many books have been written on the thoughts and perspectives around each one. The one I want to mention here is Henri Nouwen's 'wounded healer', and I think it should come with a warning sign. The idea of this model, for those unfamiliar with it, is that you share your wounds with those you are ministering to; in doing so, it forms a bond between you that helps the sufferer in the knowledge that someone else has experienced what you are going through. It is a model that I have used only twice in my ministry, and I don't like it for all the reasons I have identified in this chapter and the first chapter. In this role you are the professional. More than needing to know that you also tried to commit suicide, were an alcoholic, were abused by your partner, or had cancer, is the patient's need to know that you are spiritually holding them through their trials. It is too idealistic to think that by showing people your weakness they can find strength. But by showing your strength they can begin to believe that life might have a chance at being different.

One experience that affected me deeply and underpins my thoughts regarding the wounded healer has nothing to do with a hospital. We had been looking after my daughter's one-year-old cat, Diego, while she was on holiday. One night, late after we had gone to bed, there was a hammering at the door. A neighbour had found him lying in the gutter. He had been struck by a car. Our old cat was sitting mewing by him. We rang the emergency vet and went straight down to the surgery in our pyjamas. I loved that little cat; he was such a joy. Diego loved our old cat and followed him everywhere, evidently this night on to the main road. His back had been snapped clean in two. This meant that he was still able to move his upper body. As he lay in my arms he was crying at me, not in pain apparently, just frustrated because he could not move his legs. He put his tiny paws round my finger and looked into my eyes. He died being told how much he was loved and what a lovely cat he had been. We were completely distraught. We stood afterwards pathetically hugging each other, sobbing our hearts out. The vet was kind and compassionate. She gently led us through the process, made sure that everything was done properly and everything taken care of. She empathized with us. She did not sympathize with us, she did not join in our hug and cry with us. She did not recount a time when she had lost a cat. She was a professional, strong, efficient and kind. I felt safe in her hands that night.

It was that night that I realized that I was called to this ministry of care for the dying. What the vet had done for us that night I did for people who lost their human loved ones. I realized I was good at it, professional, that I had the personal resources to be strong and kind and compassionate to people in their most desperate times of suffering. It was what I was called to do. Not everyone can do it. Often chaplaincy is seen as an easy option for ministry. It is not. It is the hardest, most challenging ministry I have exercised, and the most fulfilling and worthwhile. It is a question you should ask yourself. Is this the ministry for you?

Conclusion

I always like the story of Simon of Cyrene. He is often missed in the busyness of Easter-week services, a small bit player in a major story. For me, it remains one of the most powerful stories in the Bible. It is one of the few times that we see Christ's weakness. Carrying his cross through the streets, being spat on, jeered at, a crown of thorns piercing his flesh, we see him stumble and fall. He can go on no longer. Simon is pulled out of the crowd. He wasn't a disciple, not one of Christ's trusted followers, but by all accounts just a person on the side-lines watching. You could say at the wrong place at the wrong time or perhaps the right place at the right time. Either way he was noticed and made to carry the cross for Jesus.

There are so many times that I see patients who are strong in faith, with the most awful stories and experiences, and they say to me, 'We never get a cross too heavy to bear.' I can say, because of Simon of Cyrene, 'Yes, we do.' Even Christ himself found it too much to bear. Just for a while he needed someone to walk beside him, holding him, loving him, until he found the strength within himself to pick himself up and continue that final road to his sacrificial death. It was to be a death that would break the mould of sin and open the gateway for all those who want to start again.

Sometimes people need permission to be weak: perhaps it is only in our weakness that we can find the strength to carry on. The throwing of ourselves before Christ, the stumbling, the falling, the weeping, the shame, the fear, are all embraced in the knowledge that through the tears and pain he will send someone to walk beside us, someone to hold us, encourage us, empathize with us, be strong for us, until we are able to dance again.

In this chapter we have looked at a tool box containing tools to enable us to be more effective communicators with patients in a hospital environment. We have considered how to be effective listeners, and how to interpret family situations. We have identified the ways in which our body language impacts on those around us, and how to overcome the most common of challenges and barriers. We have concluded with some theological reflections on the burden of suffering in our lives.

Key Points

- Listen – learn to listen and don't presume that you are a natural listener.
- Reflection – reflect back what someone has said.
- Clarification – clarify what they have said, giving them an opportunity to correct you.
- Summary – summarize in your own words what you think the situation is and what has been said.
- Interpreting situations – you only have seconds to work out family dynamics in a room. Always check what the family or patient has asked to see you for. Observe body language.
- Verbal interviewing skills – think about your tone, pitch and clarity, and don't presume all elderly people are hard of hearing.
- Questions – think about the different ways the use of questions can help your communication skills.
- Body language – be aware of your body language, both how you appear to others and reading others' body language.
- Barriers and challenges – empathy not sympathy.

5

The importance of rituals

Introduction

In this chapter we will look at the importance of rituals within a hospital setting. We will examine the differences between funeral services conducted when a patient dies within a hospital environment, without estate, and funerals in a 'normal' environment, and the pastoral implications. We will look at the practicalities surrounding baby funerals and foetal remains services. We will identify the different sacraments that a hospital chaplain or clergy may be required to perform. We will look at how we help those that are deemed 'unchurched' to find meaning through their sorrow and will consider the different ways and the adaptations that we make to worship within a hospital setting.

Funerals

When I was in circuit ministry I presided at a handful of child funerals. I am sure most clergy will agree that they are among the most distressing experiences we have as professionals. Not only are you trying to support the family and often the local community, you also have to face the emotional response in yourself when that small coffin arrives. It is at that moment when so many people are both watching you and relying on you that the enormity of the loss becomes apparent.

In a hospital situation you do not conduct many 'normal' funerals. The adult funerals are usually patients who have died without any estate and more importantly those who do not have any family or friends. When someone dies intestate the hospital will pay for their funeral out of hospital funds. The bereavement services officers make an assessment of the patient's financial situation. They contact whatever family or next of kin is available to establish if anyone can take responsibility for the cost of the funeral. If not, then the hospital pays and a chaplain is provided free of charge. The service itself is conducted with the same dignity and respect as for all other funerals. Occasionally family members will turn up or a friend or member of the community. Often it is just yourself and the funeral directors, whom I have always found to be most helpful and sensitive around these sad occasions. No organist is provided but the crematorium staff are incredibly sensitive and put on music at the beginning and end of the service.

I think it's important to know what happens so that you can, with confidence, if you are supporting a family, give them the correct information. Some families clearly have no funds available to them and you want to do the best you can for them in these circumstances. I and my colleagues always try to contact the deceased's family beforehand, or their care home or institution, and try to speak to someone who knew the person or was their key worker. Usually if you are persistent enough, even if no one on the current staff knew the person, they will have records to draw on. I always think it is worth it. You have a responsibility to the living and to the dead.

I had one experience of a lady who had learning difficulties and had been in many different care homes over the years. There were no known relatives living but there had been an announcement in the local newspaper giving information about the funeral. On the day a friend of hers from years ago was in attendance. Because I had persisted in finding out about her life I was able to weave a eulogy together that was meaningful for this lady. She wept her heart out during the service and at the end thanked me for a lovely tribute. It's easy when you are busy to cut corners and think it does not matter, but for that one lady it did.

Human nature being what it is, some people will never cease to amaze or appal you. On several occasions when office staff have asked relatives whether they can take financial responsibility for a patient's funeral, and been told that what family there is have no funds available, I have then arrived at the crematorium to find a host of family and friends with flowers and tributes. One such funeral I remember clearly. My battered old Fiat Panda was sitting outside in the car park when a fleet of Mercedes drove up the path. My little car looked lost among those new, expensive cars that surrounded it. There must have been at least 30 family and friends of the deceased arriving with lavish floral tributes. Some family members approached me and asked if they could speak or say a poem; they had even brought a grandchild with a violin to play a solo in the service. I would like to say this abuse of the bereavement service was an isolated incident but sadly it is not. It is not fair on a system that is already overstretched. I always report back to the office when it happens, and they are quite diligent in pursuing the estate to retrieve costs. However, there is no legal obligation for family members to fund the cost of a funeral. Anyone can refuse to pay for their parents', child or partner's funeral, and the cost has to be covered by the community in some way or other. Even if this is the case, the funeral service will still be conducted with the sensitivity and respect it deserves.

Baby funerals and foetal remains services

In one of the Trusts where I was a chaplain, when a mother loses a baby at the hospital or in the community there are two types of services that are available to them. If the baby was lost, for whatever reason, pre-24 weeks, they are deemed to be foetal remains. I find this term quite horrible, but it is one that everyone understands. I still think of the remains as someone's baby. These babies are put together in one coffin and several times a quarter there is a funeral service for foetal remains. The service is conducted by one of the chaplains but is closed to the public, which means parents are not in attendance. In these services there can be as many as 300 babies. The service has been written by chaplains and is not a Christian service but one that incorporates all religions and none. This was a challenge to write and the language used was difficult to agree on. On these occasions usually just the chaplain and the funeral director are present.

The baby funerals are for babies that are post-24 weeks. These babies arrive in tiny white caskets, and up to four babies are included in one service at any time. Again, the service is written by, or has an input from, all the faith chaplains or perspectives; it is for all faiths and does mention God in the language. There is a separate section around the graveside for those who do not want their baby to be included in the service, and those words do not include the word God. Recently parents have been offered the option to have a cremation on the understanding that there will be no ashes, as a baby's bones have not formed sufficiently. The babies are all buried together in a separate bay area. This is a free service offered by the hospital – I am not sure if other Trusts and councils offer this. Parents can also opt to have a private funeral that they fund themselves.

Holy Communion

There are two types of sacrament that are given in hospital. The most common one is the giving of Holy Communion. There are two ways in which this can be done. The first is at a Sunday service in the chapel. In one of the hospitals I worked at we held an ecumenical communion service. The second way is to go to the bedside and give communion on a one-to-one basis for those patients that cannot or do not want to attend the chapel for worship. When I worked in an acute large hospital there were very few attendees for the Sunday service. This was mainly because of the rapid nature of the movement of patients through the hospital. Generally if patients are well enough to attend chapel they can be moved home or to the preferred place of recovery. The way the service is conducted is slightly different in hospital. There are wafers to be distributed and a chalice with the wine. As chaplain you must wash up to your elbows before touching the elements. Those who are able are given a wafer to dip into the chalice. You must not under any circumstances allow anyone, including yourself, to drink from the chalice, owing to infection control. If you need to go to give the elements to those patients unable to come to the rail, you place the wafer in the wine then straight into their mouths without touching anything or anyone. If you unfortunately touch a patient during this process you must go back and re-clean yourself before attending to the next patient. This may sound very clinical, but the patient must come first and you cannot risk cross-infection.

In a community hospital setting it is slightly different and although there may be a chalice, you must use disposable individual communion cups that are destroyed after the service. Also, do use wafers bought from a reputable supplier. Do not bring in bread from home under any circumstances. You have a responsibility to make the distribution as infection-free as possible. Never use alcoholic wine. You do not know who you are giving communion to. It may be someone who is an alcoholic or for whom alcohol may give a reaction.

Weddings

The weddings that are performed in hospital are usually intensely emotional situations. You may have had the opportunity to get to know the couple over weeks of treatment or you may be called to the ward to give advice on the practicalities of how to go about it. Each hospital will be different, so check this out, but it is usual that none of the chaplains will be authorized to conduct the legal proceedings. However, the chaplain has another role to undertake: an administrative role. When you have talked through the situation with the patient, you must check the criteria for having a hospital wedding. Normally the doctor in attendance would need to confirm in writing that the patient is unlikely to recover and is unable to leave the hospital in order to attend the registry office in person. The patient has to be able to understand what is being said and answer appropriately, therefore they cannot be sedated or confused. It is very likely, especially in the case of an urgent situation, that you will need to chase the doctor to give you the letter. If you can, ring the registrar and give them as much information and notice as possible and fax the form through yourself so that you know that everything necessary has been done. When someone could die or slip into a coma at any moment and the decision to get married has been made, you are the key person to make sure it happens. Remember that family are trying to cope with the trauma of the news that they, or their partner, are going to die. Trying to sort out a wedding and the necessary documents may be too much for them to cope with so you need to drive it through quickly before it is too late. I have had just one experience where we did not make it in time and it was dreadful. The patient clearly wanted to make sure that his girlfriend of many years would be financially secure before he died. He slipped into a coma before the registrar arrived. A lovely gentle giant, he was only 38 years old, and his family were in conflict with him and his girlfriend. They did not resolve the family dispute either and you just knew that she was going to face a lot of conflict after he had died. As well as coping with her grief, there were several children involved and it was just a mess. I have always found registrars to be most helpful, and it is advisable to keep them in the loop at all times even if you are waiting on information to come through. As soon as everything is in place and the patient is well enough, they will come out and perform the service at a moment's notice. We then have varying levels of involvement – usually a blessing or reading – but for obvious reasons the service is usually very short.

Baptism

In the acute hospital where I worked there was a new neonatal unit. It is from this area and children's intensive care that we are usually called to perform a baby baptism. Earlier I mentioned the importance of making sure that you are prepared for what you may find when in attendance and coping with your reactions to that situation. Staff are very good at calling us in when a baby is deemed not able to survive and the parents have requested baptism. This is usually very difficult. It is never easy facing the death of a baby. Just at the point when their life should be beginning we are saying goodbye. No parent should have to say goodbye to their child. It is just wrong. There is no smart theological answer and I suggest that you do not try to give one. A bit like my vet, your job is to hold the parents emotionally when they are falling apart. If grandparents are there, they will be falling apart as well, so the normal family support mechanisms are not in place: that is your role. You need to be strong, so they can lean on your strength; be confident in your actions, kind and compassionate, and empathetic but not sympathetic. Be careful not to let the enormity of the sadness into your heart or you will not be able to fulfil your calling with integrity. To this day it is the hardest part of the job, as it should be. Most of my crying into the night is for the tiny babies not given a chance in God's beautiful world. I never ask why. Experience has taught me there is no answer.

When a baby dies on the neonatal unit, the parents are encouraged to keep a memory box, with all the things from hospital in it. The nurses will take hand and foot moulds, and a hospital photographer will come and take pictures. Expect this – you may even have to wait for the photographer to arrive. It may seem odd, and the last thing you want to do is be photographed, but this is to help the parents in the coming months and years with their grief. Years ago these babies would have been whipped away and placed in a coffin with someone unrelated to them. Evidence has taught us that the harm and damage this did to mothers could have terrible psychological consequences for the rest of their lives. So this process is in place and it seems that it goes some way in helping the parents in their grieving process. So do not smile for the camera. Just ignore it and the photographer will take sensitive shots of you, the family, the nurse and doctor. They will record all those who were part of this tiny life, to remind the family that they did exist, that we were there, that this life was not ignored or disregarded.

Meaning for the un-churched

It is often at the point of crisis that people have a question of faith. On the many occasions when there is a round of government spending cuts and chaplaincy comes under the microscope as a possible target, I think it is the 'un-churched' who would suffer the most. While people who are part of an established faith community have good pastoral visitors and clergy to visit them this is not the case for everyone, particularly young parents in my experience. These young people, when facing the death of a child, need to reach out to something – they are not sure what – to ask the difficult questions. This is often when you will be needed the most. When a parent faces losing a baby they want to know if there really is something else. They want to know if their baby will be alone, if they will see them again, if their baby will be looked after. That is what a faith offers us, confidence in life after death, of a loving God who loves and cares for all of his children. Many young people have no connection to a church, or anyone from a faith community. Can you imagine for one moment how it would feel to face the loss of a child without a faith or belief system to hold and sustain you? I actually feel I am more use in this area than any other. It is to me such an important part of my role, and the aspect that makes me want to fight to keep an active chaplaincy service as part of the National Health Service.

Worship

At some hospitals there are Sunday morning services, at others there are services throughout the week. At the acute Trust where I worked a Sunday morning ecumenical service is held to which all the patients are invited to attend. Usually there were between five and ten patients in attendance. A dedicated group of volunteers, known as the 'pushers', support patients so they can attend. They come to the hospital in time to fetch the patients from the ward in a wheelchair and take them to the service. They then sit with them through the service and make sure they are OK, then take them back to the ward. It is a secret ministry. They do not make any fuss, they turn up each week and do their task. They are a great bunch of people. Most of them started as a result of a personal experience: either of having been taken to a service by a volunteer when they had a stay in hospital and appreciating it, or when they were a patient wanting to go desperately to a service being told that the staff were too busy to take them.

Our Sunday service was a lovely little service, a bit odd with the clinical nature of the distribution of communion, but the chapel is a very spiritual place. An organist gave his time to play for the patients, which he did magnificently. It is in the Gospel of Matthew that Jesus tells his disciples not to seek glory for their work, to do it in secret almost. There was a wonderful example of secret ministry. These volunteers did not seek affirmation, or reward. Often never seeing the patients again, they just briefly touched their lives – for some of them at the bleakest moment in their lives. These people have taught me a lot about calling and working for the glory of God, not for the glory of my ego.

It is a challenge when doing a talk in services in this type of environment, as every week the themes need to be on hope and courage, and of the love of God surrounding us. You have to speak to your congregation of the day, not necessarily what the lectionary may be telling you. Also in the hymns you pick, remember who the worship is for. We would pretty much have the same hymns week in week out, old favourites that everyone knows. No one wants to finally get to the chapel only to be unfamiliar with the hymns. Again the worship is patient-led not clergy-led; it is not about you but about the patient. A lot of the patients are in pain, facing difficult truths of a long-term condition or even a terminal illness. Some cannot see, some arrive with oxygen tanks, or special devices that need plugging into the floor. It is a very different environment from a church. For starters most of the patients are in their nightdresses and pyjamas. There is something wonderful and humbling about the fact that people in their weakness, pain and suffering instinctively want to come towards God just as they are, seeking healing and comfort. It really puts into perspective the act of worship.

Of course we have had some incidents which we've laughed about later but which challenged us at the time. One day a volunteer and I went to fetch a large gentleman who came attached to his blood transfusion. Unfortunately it did not have a very long lead so we had to shuffle all the way to the chapel, which is quite a distance. On another occasion we had a lady with a catheter bag that was trailing on the floor, and a volunteer while chatting to her wheeled straight over it, drenching the chapel floor and myself with urine.

We had one patient who had been transferred onto a mobile oxygen unit to come to chapel. As we started the first hymn I noticed he was turning blue. I dashed over to find that the ward staff had not switched on the mobile cylinder. I quickly turned it on and his colour returned. As chaplain, we cannot always deal with such situations. One gentleman decided to climb out of his chair only to fall onto the floor, and the crash team were in attendance within minutes. We had to pause the service while he was attended to.

We often got patients with dementia and confusion attending the service; sometimes they had a wander around. I took one interesting service with a little lady attached to my arm throughout the proceedings. You have to take it in your stride and not be put off. I do not think we ever have a service that is 'normal'; you just have to be flexible and relaxed.

Conclusion

On reflection, in Luke we see the disciples' constant asking of Jesus what the parables mean, and he replies that to see something may not be enough and to listen to something might also not be enough. We need to be flexible in our interpretations of the stories threaded throughout the Gospels. Jesus sought ways to help the disciples understand what was needed of them and when was the time for action. Here, I think, we see the example given to us of the need to be flexible in service, always finding new ways to both minister to people and express the love of God meaningfully to really make an impact on people's lives. Jesus was always being thrown into different situations with people. Sometimes that was to test him and try to catch him out, but for as many times as we see that, we also see the people of his time, his peers, in all their wonderful uniqueness calling on him for genuine help, healing and wholeness. Jesus does not get flustered, caught out or thrown. He just takes each situation and person on its own merits without judgement and addresses the challenges of the encounter as he sees fit. In this life there is no one rule that fits all; every person is different and unique, and each situation is going to bring challenges that may push us out of our comfort zone. That is what I love most about this ministry: no two days are alike, no two encounters bring the same results and no two people think and feel the same.

In this chapter we have looked at the importance of rituals within a hospital setting and highlighted the differences to regular ministry. We have looked at the need to be flexible and ready to respond to the challenges that hospital ministry sets before you. We have examined how a hospital environment copes practically with weddings, baptisms, funerals and foetal remains. We have covered the practicalities of enabling weddings and how best to facilitate that, and considered details of how to minister sacraments and the difference in conducting worship within a hospital setting. We have looked at the important mission of reaching the un-churched with pastoral support in the difficult situations surrounding loss and letting go.

Key Points

- Funerals – hospital funerals are held when people cannot or will not finance their relative's funeral. Each funeral should be treated with dignity and respect. Try to get as much information about the deceased as possible, from whatever source.
- Baby funeral – for babies who have died post-18 weeks. Think about the words and imagery you use to incorporate all faiths and none. Candles and light are recommended and accepted by many of the faiths, making it a good universal symbol to use.
- Foetal remains services – for babies less than 18 weeks who have been miscarried or been aborted through choice or medical need. Think about language. This is still possible if you view the remains as someone's baby.
- Holy Communion – you need to completely wash up to the elbows. Keep the area clear. Distribute the wafers through tincture. Do not touch the patient when distributing; if you do, return and re-wash before administering again. Place the wafer straight into the mouth, placed upon the tongue, regardless of your own tradition. In community hospitals only use disposable individual cups, non-alcoholic wine and wafers. Do not bring bread in from your home environment, to minimize risk of infection.
- Weddings – find appropriate blessings, poems and prayers to meet a range of situations. Only those who are deemed palliative and unable to leave hospital will be allowed a hospital wedding. Good ongoing communication links are vital for a good outcome with the registrar and medical staff.

- Baptism – when called to a baby baptism it is most likely because it is not expected that the baby will live. Expect a photographer to be present. Act naturally and do not smile at the camera, but allow a record of the baptism to be recorded sensitively.
- Meaning for the un-churched – young parents losing babies often have the most probing questions to ask. Be prepared for them and have an answer that you feel has integrity and is both sensitive and compassionate. Think about the language you use, if the person is not used to theological language, so they can understand what you are saying.
- Worship – be prepared for anything to happen in a hospital. Keep the sermons short and choose hymns that are well known. Appreciate your volunteers.

6

Ministering to the care-giver

Introduction

In this chapter we will be looking at how to minister to care-givers in a healthcare environment. We seek ways in which we can minister to those who love and care for the patients and will include ways to support staff. We will look specifically at how we help care-givers to 'let go' of their loved ones. This could be either when they die, or when they have to hand over the responsibility of care to someone else. We will also look at how we really see and acknowledge the carer. The support of carers will be looked at through the use of mediation, as well as ways to support staff through counselling either in one-to-one sessions or in a group environment.

Preparing to let go

Caring for someone can be something that happens for a very short amount of time, for example while the person is recovering from an illness or operation. It can also be a dedication of duty that lasts a lifetime. This was the case with Arthur and Lily. Arthur and Lily had been married for 66 years, three months and 21 days. I can still remember that number today and this experience happened some years ago now. Arthur had looked after Lily for many years; she had had continual health problems and was confined to a wheelchair. I first knew of them long before I went off to train for ministry. They were quite a couple round where I grew up: eccentric and somewhat distinctive. Lily always had an old bobble hat on her head, and would sit clutching a cuddly toy in her wheelchair; Arthur would be dressed in the same long trench coat. They would make their way around the village where I lived, Arthur pushing Lily in her wheelchair, while she chattered away. Arthur always looked really sullen and grumpy while Lily seemed obliviously content. Now at this point I thank God for my mother, who knew and still does know everyone in the village where we grew up. My mother is a lady who stops and chats to everyone. When I was a child, we would often pause when walking into town to engage in a conversation. When we moved on I would say, 'Who was that then?' and she would reply merrily, 'No idea.' In fairness she worked at the local libraries so that is how she knew so many people at least by sight. She would often stop and chat to Arthur and Lily. I can remember her saying, 'That man is a saint.' As a young person, I admit that Arthur just looked to me like a grumpy old man. In hindsight he probably had a lot to be grumpy about. That was a long time ago; when I saw them years later in the community hospital I had to momentarily stop myself going up to them and greeting them like friends. Arthur and Lily were not religious and the call that came in one day was from the hospital matron, with whom I had built up a good relationship. She called for me out of desperation. Lily had been admitted to the hospital for rehabilitation following a hip replacement and they were having trouble with Arthur. It is interesting in itself that he should be described as 'trouble'.

When I arrived on the ward I heard the commotion long before I rounded the corner and saw the chaos. A very frail and small Lily was sitting in her wheelchair, in her nightwear, looking small and frightened. Arthur was shouting and throwing clothes into a suitcase. He was completely out of control. The matron said, 'I have called for security.' It took me some time, but I did talk him down, though not without pulling out of my arsenal all my tools. In fairness, the breakthrough came with my identifying myself as my mother's daughter, rather than as chaplain, priest or vicar. The problem was quite simply that he had felt he had lost his role with Lily, and the staff had not cared for Lily how he cared for her. This man had given his whole life to looking after his wife. The incident had erupted because the staff had combed her hair in a different style and that had tipped him over the edge. It was loss of control, loss of identity and his suppressed feelings coming to the surface. He was frightened. Arthur thought he was losing Lily and that meant losing his identity, everything he was as a person, a carer, husband and friend.

Elisabeth Kübler-Ross has identified the five stages of grief as denial, anger, bargaining, depression and acceptance, stages that have been expanded on by other professionals. The hypothesis is that when a person is faced with the reality of impending death, or another extreme source of loss, they will experience a series of emotional stages. In the context of the hospital environment it is important to remember that the grief cycle can begin long before the prospect of death is present. The same feelings of loss can come at the breakdown of a relationship or in the loss of a role. When we are ministering to patients it is easy to forget the needs and feelings of those who have cared for the patient long before the hospital and staff intervened. Learning to really see a person, in a full and rounded way, helps us to capture the moment that our paths cross, and understanding the whole person can aid in the healing process. This will be discussed further in the next section.

Seeing the carer in an alien environment

How we treat another human being when they are in crisis says more about ourselves than it does about them. The ability to be able to really see someone, see who they are, among all the trapping and labels we as a society and culture place on them, is a challenge. We often see what we want to see. As Christian people we have at the heart of our gospel a call not to judge, but to love. How many of us can say we achieve that? We come to people with preconceptions and judgements. I think it is better to accept it and acknowledge it, allowing you to modify your behaviour accordingly, than try to deny it. It is the thing I most hate about myself. When I catch myself judging or labelling someone, I am always really hard on myself for it, so acknowledge it and try to reassess.

We can never really know what experiences have shaped and moulded someone else's life and experience. We may not know who loves them or who has loved them. We cannot be sure if they are alone in the world, or know what sort of house they live in, or what is important to them, unless they choose to disclose it to us. I think the greatest privilege of this role is the chance to get to know people, walk with them emotionally for a while and share with them some precious moments, albeit in a time of great sadness.

Not many things get me really angry these days. I try to remain calm and understanding about most things. However, someone mocking another human being or making a spontaneous value judgement about them will cause a surge of anger in me every single time. I would like to share with you the story of Joan as an example of what makes me angry.

I was called into the acute hospital as chaplain on call for a patient on the Liverpool Care Pathway. The nurse in charge said it was for the daughter of the patient who was dying, who she felt needed pastoral support. It was four o'clock in the morning and I had been woken from a dead sleep, and even the tea I drank in the car on the way to the hospital had not really defuddled my brain. By the time I arrived on the ward the nurse on duty had swapped over and another young nurse was in charge. I asked to see the patient's daughter and was shown onto the ward. The patient was dying behind a curtain in a ward that was far from ideal, but often a reality. As she pulled the curtain back – I will never forget my anger – the young nurse smirked at me and said, 'Hope you're ready for this.' Joan, the daughter, sat there holding her father's hand, crying softly. I introduced myself to her. She was so distraught that I went over and gave her a hug. We sat and chatted while the dawn was breaking. Joan was a transsexual and, at a guess, I would say somewhere in her late 50s. She was awaiting surgery and was dressed in 1940s ladies' clothes. Her make-up was crude and her hair styled in quite an outdated style. During those hours together she told me about her life, that she had cared for her father, and for her mother who was disabled and had dementia. She told me of the rejection of the rest of her family and how she had no real friends or support mechanisms. Joan told me how people ridiculed her. She had even been spat at in the street. During this time, she gently wiped her father's brow, kept telling him she loved him and reassuring him that she would never leave him. She was full of apologies for getting me out of bed in the middle of the night and was a gentle, kind person. I was so moved; she had so much love in her heart, yet had faced so much pain. Joan was trying to be who she believed she was. Life is often complex. What I saw was a beautiful person trapped in a man's body. I cannot imagine how that must have felt, but as human to human we held each other's hands as her father died. Two human beings: one shared humanity.

The real intimacy for me was in that after her father died, she did not want to pull back the curtain. Joan had noticed the look the nurses had given her and she was worried about her make-up having rubbed off her face through the continual crying and it now not covering her stubble. I got a bowl of warm water and a cloth and, in the silence of the breaking dawn, washed her face and reapplied her make-up for her. I am a woman who wears make-up and there was something so powerful in sharing that time, helping her to re-establish her identity before facing the world and all the grief and pains she now had to face.

How often do we really see someone, who they are, who loves them, what makes their life worth living? How often do we appreciate the privilege of sharing in another person's life, albeit for a few hours, with all its complexities and perhaps without being able to fully understand? If you remember one thing from this book, it is never to think that you have seen and experienced everything. We cannot understand everything;

some questions just have to sit with us unanswered. Be content in that.

How we treat people says so much about ourselves. We bring to our role all sorts of misconceptions, prejudice and habits from our socialization. To treat people with respect and dignity we first must become fully aware of our own behaviour. If we add the filter of our theology, we have a challenge. This is a high calling on our lives.

Supporting parents with a terminally ill child

In the context of a hospital environment, dealings with children can be very difficult. I am not sure if having your own children makes this a harder job or an easier one. I know, after the experiences of this role, never to take for granted my children, and my ability to have had my children when I wanted them. I hope it makes me more empathic but I am always learning new things about myself and my role. There are some skills that are particularly useful when supporting parents of children with different family dynamics.

First, lesbian or gay parents; I'm putting this first because it is the one that is most often forgotten about unless it is part of your psyche for another reason. Do not presume that the children you are visiting have a mum and dad. They may have two mums or two dads. If so, their experience will already have likely met with prejudice through the system. Not making assumptions can help with relationship-building later down the line.

Single parents can need a different kind of support from when a child has two parents. Single parents need a great deal of emotional support particularly if operations and test results are coming up. Making a note of important markers in their child's process and going onto the ward to follow up on those days is really helpful. This is important to all parents but those coping alone are more likely to need someone on those occasions. If you are not a parent, get some storybooks and practise reading aloud using funny voices until you are comfortable doing it. Also a little hand-puppet is invaluable; develop a name and character for it. The child will ask if you have brought it with you and it will help to establish a relationship. It will become something that the two of you can share together. This means that you can offer practical help, such as sitting with the child while Mum has a shower or pops to the canteen for something to eat.

There are many different scenarios to consider, such as when the parent has a disability or the child has a disability, or if the family are non-English speaking and the child is the interpreter. This is where working as part of a multifaith team is useful, and having a variety of volunteers representing different faiths and different cultural backgrounds is a vital tool to good communication and support.

In the next chapter we will cover the impact of truth-telling. When you are supporting families and it concerns children it is slightly different, though, so I mention it separately now as it directly impacts on supporting the carer in this context. Often when a family is caring for a child, there can be no other option when it comes to truth-telling but to keep a conspiracy of silence; the parents may be in denial, or not wanting to discuss the reality of their situation. Never in my experience has a family ever given up on a child, not until they have actually died. Right up to the last moment when they close their eyes for the last time, everyone usually remains hopeful and does not want to discuss the what ifs. I think it is important that the chaplain, priest or volunteer also takes on that mantle, however remote the possibility. It is where I have seen the most miracles and the occasions I save my most desperate prayers for. If I am asked directly by the parents what I think will happen I say something like, 'I have seen the most miracles with children. I am not going to give up, you must not either. Come on, we both need to be strong.'

When supporting a family we are often called to say a prayer and I am a great fan of spontaneous prayers. Remember that they may not be church people and have little expectation or understanding of liturgy. I would like to encourage you to say what you feel – be brave. It is easy to hide behind a book or sheet; I think it is far more appreciated if you speak from the heart. If you are not very good at this, practise. Touching the child (with consent) and praying from the heart, not stopping and finding a pre-written prayer, is the most effective ministry. Make sure you get not only the names of the parents but what they like to be called and use their names as well. It is so much more personal. Search for the intimacy of the relationship. Remember they are in an alien environment. Their baby is often being prodded and pulled, or full of tubes, and they are being talked to in a clinical way about the most precious life they have created. Find the humanness in the connection.

The use of touch has been discussed earlier in this book and any touch always needs to have verbal consent. All healthcare staff need to get consent, even if that consent is verbal, before any procedure on a patient, and it is the same for us. Always ask if you can hold their hand, or hold their baby. I always ask to hold babies, particularly when they have died. I always kiss their precious little heads, and, as mentioned in a previous chapter, it can be a disturbing vision. Never lose sight of the parents. It is their baby. Would you want someone to touch your baby without asking? If you have not held a tiny baby before or in a while, go to the maternity ward and ask to hold one. Or perhaps you have a friend who has a new baby. The more healthy babies you handle, the better skilled you will be with the tiny ones you will come across in the hospital. Do not let fear become a barrier to your success.

Hugging is one kind of touching that often goes a long way; although if you are male, you might want to think through carefully its consequences – sadly that is the world in which we live now. Allowing parents or carers to cry on your shoulder, or, gaining consent first, holding their hand or giving them a hug is a very powerful ministering tool. It never ceases to amaze me how little we physically touch each other. I am fortunate enough to have someone who loves me and will give me a hug when I am feeling low or lost. Imagine how you would feel if you had to watch your child go into surgery and there was no one in your life to put their arms around your shoulders. I was for many years a single parent and I will never forget when my son went in for a minor op and my mum needed to stay with my daughter. I remember standing in the hospital corridor with his trainers in my hand feeling absolutely desperate and that there was no one there for me. Try to think – how would I feel? What would I benefit from right now?

Long-term carers of children often find that the practicalities of life get in the way of what they might need or want. I have had several cases where one of a child's parents has had to go back to work and the other spends most nights on a cot in the room with the child. This is very isolating and often causes tensions and frictions within their relationship. A listening ear and friend to accompany them on the long journey is a really important support mechanism. An offer to sit with the child or baby while Mum or Dad goes for a break is a helpful, practical way to exercise your ministry and a really good opportunity for a volunteer role.

I have had some of my most profound conversations with parents when the danger time is over and the long road to recovery has started, when they start to process what has happened to them. Coming through the danger period is not the end: it is the beginning of a new journey. They find the challenge of isolation and long-term caring quite demanding as the normal support systems like grandparents and friends and family are not there. This is where the ability to accompany them for the long haul comes into its own. Supporting long-term carers is really important, but we must not forget the carers who are caring for patients day in, day out: the staff.

Staff support

There are several ways in which we can support staff; the first is on a one-to-one basis. If you have completed any counselling training, this is where it comes into its own. To provide a 'safe space' where staff can come and off-load is an important service. Establishing relationships so that staff know the service is there can be a little more challenging. Often it is word of mouth. In the office of the acute hospital where I worked there was a small 'dignity' room. Staff would sometimes go there and just burst into tears as an outlet to a situation that had occurred on the ward. The ability to respond quickly is vital. If you are not trained in counselling, fear not. All that may be needed is the offer of a cup of tea and a listening ear. Staff in the NHS are under enormous stress through budget cuts and job pressures. It can be a tinder box, with emotions running high, and often a row will emerge. The role of the chaplain or volunteer is to be listener, negotiator and facilitator. To enable the process – this is just a personal view – never get too close to ward staff. The reason for this is that if you are visibly friendly with some staff and not others, it will put people off seeking you out to talk to. They will not come to you if they think you are best friends with the ward matron. Trust is the most important element of the relationship. You will have little opportunity to change what is happening – if they are understaffed or someone is picking on them or a family have taken out their frustrations on them. Offering an empathic listening ear will go a long way to getting things back on track and making the staff feel supported. Another route of support is group support.

Group support

From time to time we are called in to address an issue that has manifested itself in a way that is hampering the ward or office area. One of these occasions was a call to an admin office in the hospital. All the staff in the office had experienced bereavement within a few weeks and somehow they had managed collectively to convince themselves that the room was haunted. They wanted some sort of exorcism. Now this is not as rare as you might imagine, although this particular situation was. Often with regard to exorcism we will be called to a particular ward or a room where there have been several deaths. Staff and families begin to believe that the room is haunted and want, in their terms, an exorcism. On a child's oncology ward, there are sadly going to be quite a few deaths and, as with the neonatal ward, one room is put aside for the withdrawal of treatment. Therefore that is the room where most of the babies and children die. In my view this is not a theological issue but a pastoral one, and you should handle it pastorally, not necessarily theologically. Treat the system not the cause.

With regard to the admin office, we went to talk to the group, who had got to a point of near hysteria about the room. We talked through exactly what they thought was going on and why. Most importantly we asked them what they thought would make them feel more peaceful. I am sure, to this day, one of them had seen something on television that had triggered these thoughts as it seemed to be supposition. Rather than tell them not to be silly, or how it was just coincidence, we tackled the symptom. They wanted us to complete an exorcism. We explored with them what they thought an exorcism was: it was a priest (us) saying prayers round the room. This we could do quite easily. The Church of England has a liturgy for this occasion which you can use; alternatively, I have included my own versions at the back of the book for you to use. We completed the prayers as requested and they visibly relaxed and were able to get on with their jobs.

Often the words people use and what they mean do not tally. It is a good idea to explore with people when they have asked for something what exactly they think that entails. If you have a situation where ward staff or patients say that things get smashed or moved when no one is there, it is slightly different. This can be a challenge to you theologically, if they really believe that there is a force in the room that means harm to people. I would advise that you do not undergo any ritual of this nature alone; do it with someone else. Whatever you may or may not believe theologically, I personally never underestimate a situation or think, as I said earlier, that I have seen everything and understand everything. There are things in this universe that we do not understand. Precautions should be taken for yourself and your colleagues.

Conclusion

There are so many examples of Jesus supporting the carer in the Gospels that it is impossible to pick just one story to identify with. We see the importance Jesus placed on allowing people to care for him, for example when he went to the home of Mary and Martha, both in the practical sense of hospitality and the spiritual sense of Mary anointing his feet. We see Jesus rebuking the disciples when people tried to bring children to Jesus, presumably parents wanting either healing or a blessing on their children's lives. However, it is the story of Zacchaeus that resonates with me the most. Whatever else we have learnt from this chapter, we need to understand the importance of seeing and accepting someone as they are and supporting them in that role, even if at first we cannot understand them or feel we have inadequate skills to do so. Zacchaeus was a man who had lost his way, a corrupt tax collector, following the wrong path. Yet in the instant that Jesus looked up and saw him, he really saw him, saw into his heart and called him by name. He gave him a chance when others turned away. It epitomizes this ministry for me: that we are there for the lost, the broken, for those who have gone astray, who others turn away from.

In this chapter we have looked at how the role of chaplain can offer support to those who are care-givers: relatives, friends and staff. We have considered how to support carers who have to say goodbye to their responsibilities of caring either for a short while or permanently, how to recognize and support people who are struggling with isolation and how to really see people as human beings while understanding who they are. We have explored how to support staff on a one-to-one basis and as part of a group experience, and how to cope when ward areas or rooms become a barrier to patients and staff delivering the appropriate care to patients.

Key Points

- People have to let go not only in death but also in giving over responsibility of care. The emotions are the same as bereavement and should be supported thus.
- Really seeing the carer, not just the patient or service-user, and supporting them is really important. Even if you do not understand or agree with someone's life choices they deserve the same support and encouragement.
- When supporting parents be prepared for a long relationship. Practical support may be just as vital as spiritual support.
- Buy a few pop-up books and practise reading stories with different voices. A small glove-puppet could be your best friend!
- When supporting staff, be seen as independent of ward politics.
- Always gain consent before touching a patient, but it is a powerful comfort support.
- Practise holding babies.
- When completing exorcisms or cleansing rituals, always work in pairs.

7

Helping people face difficult truths – whose truth is it?

Introduction

In this chapter we will look at the complexities surrounding truth-telling in a clinical environment. Ways in which we can tackle situations when families hold a conspiracy of silence and what that means will be discussed. The way in which we as pastoral care-givers can support patients when they receive bad news – and how we cope with the situation when the patient does not want to know the truth – will be looked at.

Truth-telling in a clinical environment

Some time ago now I attended a training day for pastoral visitors and the visiting speaker was a consultant in palliative care from a local hospice. As is the fashion, the speaker asked what we wanted to learn from the day and requested a list of topics that we could cover and explore during the session. So as usual at these events, people started to raise their hands and ask for different topics to be covered, with nods of approval from the floor. I duly raised my hand and asked that we cover 'truth-telling'. You could have heard a pin drop; the room went deadly silent. The consultant delivered a tight-lipped grimace and placed it on the flip chart at the bottom and moved on. A moment's pause of silence in the room sounded louder than a herd of elephants stampeding through a city street! Truth-telling never did get covered that day. I was to find out that it is a very contentious issue within healthcare circles. This is mainly because it is so subjective and personal. On reflection I believe this is because like most events involved in clinical encounters there is not a master guide that fits all situations. Humans are unique individuals and so each one's situation is uniquely individual. The textbook answer, for clinicians, is that if a patient asks directly they should be told the truth. The problem is then, 'What is the truth?' We come from a tradition that places a high value on 'the truth', but what is the truth for one person may not be the truth for another. What might be helpful here is to exchange the word 'truth' for 'honest information-giving'.

Each clinician has to make a clinical judgement call for the betterment of their patient, without the religious connections associated with honest information-giving. To tell a patient they are going to die, or that nothing more can be done for them and they are withdrawing active treatment, brings with it the possibilities that the patient will get depressed, give up, lose any sense of hope or purpose and may attempt to take their own life. Equally there are those patients who want to know so that they can make appropriate provisions and arrangements.

John was one such complex situation. John was a 35-year-old ex-marine and police officer. He was an intelligent man who had asked to see the chaplain. John was completely paralysed when I met him and wearing a 'halo', which is a contraption used when a back or neck is broken. It is very heavy and uncomfortable, and movement is very limited in it. John was lying on his back unable to move, and unresponsive. Our relationship lasted the nine months of his stay, and it was not easy for either of us. To begin with his only acknowledgement of me in the room was that he would look at me. He refused to speak and I was to learn that his admission was due to an attempted suicide that had gone wrong. It is really hard to make a relationship with someone who will not speak to you. As a chaplain or visitor, you do not want to force yourself on the patient and in John's case he was completely helpless. I was aware that I was the one with the power. I had the power to come and go, to choose what I said or not. Yet he had made the request initially to see me, so even though I did not feel I was getting very far I persevered with visiting him, getting little or no response.

It was the remembrance service that was my breakthrough. He was watching it on a small television in his room and I went to speak to him, as usual gaining no response. As I looked down I noticed he was crying. I touched his hand and he simply said, 'Sit down . . . please.' I did, and a relationship grew from that moment. Many people would have given up on him; as it happens many people had given up on him in his life. I just stuck in there believing that I had a role in this part of his journey but not sure what that would be.

John was a really interesting spiritual man who had travelled the world as a marine. He told me about the temples and places of worship all over the world he had visited whenever he was sent on missions. The stories were vivid and colourful and in the cold winter months, when he lay in the darkness of his room unable to move, those stories filled our afternoons with excitement and magic. John told me that while in the marines he had been given inoculations for special operations that had caused his severe depression and made him want to take his own life. He was a man who knew he had mental health problems; he was intelligent and rounded as a human being. Eventually the clinicians began piecing him back together and the extent of the damage was realized.

It was me that the ward staff called after the truth about his condition had been told to John. The doctors had told him the damage was irreparable and that he would forever be paralysed from the waist down. Never underestimate someone with mental-health issues. I have never witnessed a scene like the one I was called to. The police were outside the room when I arrived, as well as security. They had evacuated the ward. John was threatening to kill himself and had already damaged himself, so the doctors desperately needed to get to him. I was allowed by John to go into his room. He had unscrewed the light bulb from the lamp above his head and he had slashed his neck and wrists. There was blood all over the walls and covering the bed. He was threatening to push it into his neck if anyone else came in. I persuaded him to give it to me and the doctors came and ministered to his wounds.

He could not cope with the 'truth' of his situation. Yet he had asked a direct question and been given honest information. When people talk about 'rights' it is important to remember that when you are giving information, or acknowledging a truth, you have a responsibility which could have ramifications that you could not begin to imagine.

It is at this point that I want to raise the issue of mental health, although I will cover this in more depth in Chapter 9. It seems appropriate in the section on truth-telling. At the beginning of my chaplaincy it was the area that most frightened me. It was not because I was afraid of what sights I might witness or what might be said to me; I was worried about not being able to know if someone was telling me the truth or not or of being 'taken in'. Now far more experienced, I realize it is not a problem for me at all. I do not know if John was an ex-marine and if he went to all those places he told me about. What was important was that in that moment I entered into his world without suspicion or accusation and shared in his life.

As a child I used to watch *Mr Benn*, a lunch-time cartoon. He was a man dressed in a suit and bowler hat, and he had a briefcase. Mr Benn went, on his lunch breaks, to a little fancy dress shop. Each day he tried on a different outfit. He then went out of the changing rooms at the back of the shop and entered into the world that suited his outfit and had an adventure. He then returned to the changing room and put his suit on again at the end of the programme and went back to his office. That is the best description I can give you of supporting a patient with mental-health challenges. It is not your place to decide what is happening to them. Their truth is their truth. It may not be your truth. You enter into their world and journey with them, sometimes to colourful, vibrant places that are a lot better than the reality of their ordinary world. Sometimes you accompany people in the darkness and loneliness of their truth, then like Mr Benn you come back out, put on your suit and go back to work. You do not have to work out what is real and what is not. The encounter was real. Your support was real. The relationship that you have established is real. They are the truths that you need concern yourself with. Leave the rest to the clinicians.

Many patients are seeking answers to questions. I try to answer all questions that are asked of me as honestly as I can and many, many people ask me if they are going to die. In terms of truth-telling, it could be said that it is the only one real truth there is; that we are all going to die. Try to look behind the question and the reason why someone wants to know the answer to that particular question. I have had the good fortune to have worked with an excellent palliative care team. This team was led by a consultant in palliative care and consists of the consultant, registrar and specialist nurses, and a chaplain. This relatively small team of people are dedicated to making sure that all those patients who are deemed terminal and are put on palliative care die without pain and suffering, and with dignity and respect. There are weekly meetings to discuss the palliative patients that have been referred to the team in the hospital. Each patient is recounted and their symptoms and problems are discussed. It never ceases to amaze me that in an age when pods are being sent to Mars we still cannot determine when someone is actually going to die. Only God knows that. What is important is to understand why someone wants to know if they are going to die and what are they going to do once they know. That really is when our work begins with spiritual care.

Sometimes patients want to know the truth about whether they are going to die for practical reasons. I have been present at many weddings where people's primary concern is to provide security for their loved ones. We have helped in the practicalities of getting solicitors in and organizing wills for people. As a team we have been called in as scribes for letter-writing for patients attempting to repent and gain forgiveness for past wrongs. Not everyone talks in theological language but a common theme keeps presenting itself surrounding guilt, forgiveness and peace.

When the family hold a conspiracy of silence

As stated in the previous section, the art of truth-telling has many pitfalls. One of the difficulties that healthcare staff, including chaplains, come across regularly is when the family are holding a conspiracy of silence. This is usually with the very best intentions. Some or all family members do not want the medical staff to tell their mum, dad or partner that the news is bad. They are often worried about how they will react, for all the reasons mentioned at the beginning of this chapter. Sometimes when we take away someone's hope, the light within them just dims and grows weaker: a kind of giving up. To the family, this seems avoidable. Some families want to keep up the stoical attitude that he/she will be all right. It is at these points that you have to ask if this attitude is really for the patient or whether it is a way for the family and loved ones to cope.

I was called one Saturday afternoon to one of the hospitals that I cover to see a big bear of a man who had been brought to the hospital for an ECMO (extracorporeal membrane oxygenation). Part of intensive-care medicine, it is a technique of providing both cardiac and respiratory support oxygen to patients whose heart and lungs are so severely diseased or damaged that they can no longer serve their function. Basically it is used as a last attempt to give the patient a chance of recovery. It takes the blood out of the person, puts it through a cleanser and then puts it back into the body. For the patient it looks a bit like something from a futuristic movie and it is not a very pleasant experience for the family and relatives to watch.

On this occasion the family, who were from an evangelical tradition, were in attendance around the bed. The staff told me that the ECMO had not worked and the patient was at the end of his life. I went in to see the patient, who was unconscious, and introduced myself to the family. One of the daughters was chanting in the corner, rubbing his arm. There was another daughter rubbing his legs and feet. They were all united in an almost hysterical refrain: 'Come on, Dad, you can do it.' I asked gently what they were willing their father to do. 'Live,' they said. I asked what they would like me to do and they said to pray for a miracle. My silent prayer was indeed for a miracle, not for the man to live, because quite clearly it was time for his earthly life to end, having no brain response, but a miracle of another sort. I prayed that before he died I could get this loving family to let him go, to see that God's hand was upon this man, and his soul safely in God's hands. For him to die peacefully they needed to stop the hysteria of trying to stop death. In the fight for his life they were shutting out the important emotional engagement with the sentiments he needed to hear. I was granted a miracle that day. The patient lasted two hours and I used every minute of that precious time to help them release the grip of love that was suffocating him and replace it with calm and peace. I encouraged them to talk of the joys and memories that he had given them and that they would treasure all their lives. I got them to talk about how good a father, husband and grandfather he was. Finally I asked them to tell him that he could go to his Father with their blessing. I felt the presence of God in the room with me that day, standing in the corner, arms outstretched calming the storm. It was a storm that had blown up from desperation and love trying to keep hold of that which was most precious and, in doing so, denying the inevitable.

When the patient doesn't want to know

Hope is an unfathomable entity, and patients and their conditions are all so different that I could not begin to categorize those patients who will want to know the truth of their situation and those who will not. There are those who are told, but clearly cannot or will not hear. I think the key to these reactions is in the concept of hope. During the season of

Advent there is often a focus on hope. We can use this theme to help patients in their time of waiting, whatever that waiting may be for. It is often in the waiting that we face ourselves in the purest and most stripped-back sense. When there is nothing but hope we look into the mirror of our lives and assess who and what we are and how we can, with help, be different.

Every so often you come across a patient who really gets into your psyche and you end up, psychologically, taking them home. You tell your loved ones about them, you think about them and sometimes they haunt your dreams. You never know which are the ones who will infiltrate your protective psychological barriers, it just happens. You are human, not divine; prepare yourself for this, because it will happen and it will hurt. One such case was baby Harry. I had been called to the children's emergency care unit and asked to baptize Harry. He was two years old and looked quite healthy compared with most of the children we see on the wards. He had a cheeky smile and a twinkle in his eyes. He also had a rare aggressive form of cancer; the tumour had grown rapidly within two weeks and had consumed the entire inside cavity of his upper torso. There was little chance of survival. Harry's parents had asked not to know the prognosis; they needed to believe he would get better; they needed to have their hope remain intact. The parents were self-confessed 'not religious', which is quite common, but wanted all the help they could get from a God that may or may not exist. I baptized Harry. As is usual following a baptism, I kept in close contact with the family, and Harry went through the rounds of chemo in an attempt to reduce the tumour. They began asking me to say 'a little prayer' before I left. Harry's dad said that they had been going to the chapel at night to sit and think.

When the day came that the surgeon said he was prepared to risk surgery, Harry's parents asked me to pray for him. I asked everyone I knew to pray that day. He had won my heart with his strength and determination to fight. When I left him as he went into theatre he waved goodbye to me and smiled through his mask; I knew then that I may never see him again and it broke my heart. I knew then why his mum and dad had refused to listen to percentages of survival rates. Instead they chose to trust in a God of hope, a God that never gives up on us even though we may give up on him. I surrendered my heart to that little boy and prayed that he would return. Return he did.

Equally there are many examples of patients who want to be told the truth of their situation so that they can 'get their house in order'. I was visiting two women on the haematology ward. They were in beds next to each other. On the same day the consultant had to speak to each woman and tell her that the treatment had not been successful. In both cases there was only one course of action available to them. The treatments were the same via a new trial drug. The drug came with uncertainties and, as is the nature of trials, could be unpredictable. They were told that the success rate was 10 per cent. This was an unprecedented case on the ward; all the staff were deeply affected, and patients and staff on the ward needed a lot of support during the process. One of the women said that 10 per cent was not a good enough chance to risk the side effects and decided to go home and be with her family for as long as she could. The other decided that 10 per cent offered enough hope to take the risk and she prepared herself to start the treatment. Supporting those patients at the same time, while they came to make those really important decisions, was difficult because it brought into question how we cling to hope, and what we do in the absence of hope. The lady that stayed for the treatment died two days later having contracted an infection. I do not know how long the other lady had at home with her family. I hope she had long enough to do and say all she wanted to before saying goodbye to those she loved.

Conclusion

Hope gives us a reason to carry on, not to give up, and to be strong and brave. Hope fills the gaps of pain and accompanies us through the darkness of waiting. A life without hope is a life without breath. Yet sometimes it allows us to hide in the shadow and not face the truths of situations as they are. It is in his first letter to the Corinthians (1 Cor. 13) that Paul writes of love being the most significant of all emotions; in the most famous paragraph he talks of faith, hope and love but that it is love that surpasses all things. There is a time for all things, as we are told in Ecclesiastes. There is a time for hope and there is a time to let hope go and give over to the love of God, knowing and understanding that the love of God will encompass all things. The handing over of hope is the handing over of control of our lives and will to God, and only in the surrendering of ourselves can we be truly at peace. There is a time to fight and a time to give in; let God do the fighting for us.

In this chapter we have looked at what truth-telling means in a clinical environment and the challenges that clinicians and pastoral visitors face when answering difficult questions. We have explored why families might want to hold a conspiracy of silence and what we can and should do if we are faced with that dilemma. We have looked at how to support patients who do not want to know bad news, and those who do want to know the truth and how they face the choices that are available to them in those circumstances. We have ended by looking at the role of hope within truth-telling.

Key Points

- Truth-telling should be treated with caution as it has many ramifications.
- Understanding why someone wants to know the truth or not is helpful in aiding the pastoral support process.
- When you enter into an encounter with a patient, you enter into their world and their truth.
- No one actually knows when someone is going to die – only God knows that. There are, however, medical signs to indicate that the end of life is approaching.

- Practically helping a patient or family to prepare to die or let go of a loved one is a valuable part of our role.
- Sometimes truth goes into direct conflict with hope. Be careful when handling situations like these, particularly surrounding children.

8

Dying matters

Introduction

In this chapter we will look at the difficult topic of dying. We will analyse the implementation of the Liverpool Care Pathway in light of current negative media coverage. We will address the way in which we can support staff, patients and families when making difficult decisions in a clinical environment. We will look at how people cope with the fear of dying and consider the practicalities of when someone actually dies.

Liverpool Care Pathway – the concept

The title of this chapter is 'Dying matters' because I believe passionately that dying really does matter and it is something that as a society, generally speaking, we do not do well. There are some good reasons for this but it needs addressing at every level. Recently in the media, there has been negative coverage surrounding the Liverpool Care Pathway (LCP), a system of care for those at the end of life, and at the time of writing many hospitals are withdrawing the use of it or considering its future. The media has for the most part portrayed the pathway negatively, which has frightened people who have relatives on the pathway or nearing end of life. I have found this very frustrating. Families resist agreeing to their loved ones being cared for using the pathway because of what they have read or heard in newspapers and on television. The LCP was introduced as a direct response to some of the horror stories that were coming out from family and patient experiences when coming to the end of life. The idea in its simplest form is that when a patient is deemed to be dying, when they are at the end of their life and no more effective treatment is available to them, they are cared for using the LCP, where medication is withdrawn in favour of purely palliative care. This is usually within the last 24–72 hours of life and has several benefits. On a purely practical note for the hospital staff, rather than many different departments keeping their own records on the patients, all the record-keeping from that moment comes together into one document. This is placed onto the front of the patient notes. Therefore any communications between different disciplines is easily accessible and nothing gets missed. In practical terms for the patient, regular tests and invasive treatments may be considered inappropriate. When a patient is in the last 24 hours of life, the body starts shutting down and food and water may be refused, which is all part of the natural process of dying. However, I and my colleagues have been aware of patients being shaken awake by healthcare assistants because the family had insisted that he/she needed to eat to get better. On many occasions when I have been sitting quietly with a dying person, when all that is needed is peace and quiet, the door bangs open and a jolly healthcare assistant shouts, 'Morning John, how about a nice cup of tea?' This is totally inappropriate, yet regularly experienced. It is the same with medication and blood pressure checks.

I had been visiting a 94-year-old lady who had been poorly for some time. Her daughter had read the latest newspaper scare-mongering and when the doctors suggested caring for her using the LCP, the daughter disagreed. While I was with the lady, reading the Psalms quietly, just before she died, we were disturbed several times: once for a blood pressure test, once for a finger prick for her diabetes and once for a nurse attempting to give her a warfarin tablet when she was unconscious. The nurse actually stood there pondering how to get her medication down her! You cannot blame the staff. They have got to do their job, which unless the patient is being cared for using the

LCP means that active treatment is usually continued. Particularly in the current blame culture staff need to operate by the book, but in terms of patient welfare it can be awful to watch. This little bird-like lady who had come to terms with dying was pushed and prodded in her final hours when she could have easily been left quietly to die peacefully. Whatever replaces the LCP should be supported as there needs to be something that aids a patient in the last stages of life to have their wishes respected. The root of the problem cannot be solely laid at the doorstep of the media, though they have a lot to answer for. The problem lies much deeper in our psyche, and it is to do with dying and not accepting death as part of the life cycle. We almost have a collective obsession with trying to elude death, rather than embracing it and making sure it is experienced with grace and dignity.

Difficult conversations

There is a charity project in which I have played an active part called Dying Matters. It encourages people to have those difficult conversations early in their lives rather than leaving it until the end, when it may be too painful for people to hear. Everyone needs to embrace talking about death as a normal part of our lives rather than shutting it out in the coal shed in the hope that it won't come banging on the door, asking for entry. Death is going to happen to each and every one of us. There's no escaping it, no denying it; it is the one certainty we have in life. So why do we refuse to speak about it? I was the worst offender until I started in this post and saw the importance of honest conversations.

My mother has for years been prepared for dying. She has a silver box. It has her will and her funeral service planned out within it. For years when she tried to speak to me about it I avoided it, telling her to stop being morbid, or simply pushed the thought to the back of my mind and changed the subject. I was wrong; she was right. It is important for her to be able to express that she is aware that her life has a limit to it. In wanting to talk to me about it she is expressing that she wants us (me and my sisters) to be without hassle and to be looked after when she does die. She is expressing a maternal love for us that encompasses earthly life and embraces eternity. As in her life here on earth, she wants our future to be as painless and free of burden as she can make it. For me to ignore or, worse, dismiss that concern could be considered disrespectful and unfair. I know I am being hard on myself and that there are good reasons why I and others will have taken this path. I do not want to lose her from my life and the thought of her dying is difficult for me to come to terms with, so I would rather make light and ignore it. In doing so I am ignoring her need to be spiritually at peace. She is a woman who has been organized all her life; it is only right that she would want to leave her earthly life neatly and with everything in order. I have now changed. I now speak about death intrinsically linked with living. In this way it is not morbid. I want to openly encourage people to have those conversations with their loved ones before they are on their death-beds, and in doing so we can share the memories and meanings in the choices and preparations that we make.

An example of this was one lady that I saw on the wards, Maureen. Often patients know when they are going to die even if there has been no formal notification of it. People will ask me to scribe what they want for their funerals. It is a great privilege to share this moment with patients. They ask me to write down what they would like and during the conversation they will tell me why they want a particular hymn and what a special reading means to them. Maureen was one of those patients. The ward rang the office requesting a Methodist. That is actually very unusual, as people in hospital do not normally see barriers of denominations, but Maureen had asked for a Methodist and I duly went along. She wanted a scribe for her funeral. We went through the Methodist hymn books and I sang out some hymns to remind her of the tunes; she had been a soloist in her day and she tried to sing along with me. We had a wonderful morning together. She told me that after her mother died, she found her hymn book with two hymns ticked, and she picked them for the funeral; and she decided to have them at her funeral as well. At the end of the session she asked me to hide the piece of paper in her bag, somewhere where her girls would find it after she died. She did not want to upset them by talking about it. The next morning she died. Her daughters had missed that beautiful conversation and time of singing together because of a taboo around death.

I have written down, and told my children, what I want for my funeral. To be honest they roll their eyes at me, but they know that death is part of life and that no conversation is out of bounds; there is nothing that they cannot talk about with me. Like most difficult conversations, if we set an example by being honest and open in our reactions to death, people will know they can talk to us about it. If they can talk to us, they can perhaps take the next step and talk to those they love. My experience has been that the families who have had those difficult conversations cope so much better with the grieving process because they do not have inter-family conflicts, nor do they have the burden of guilt over whether they have made the right decision.

Dealing with fear

As a specialist in palliative care, one of the main questions I get asked is, 'What do you say to people who are frightened of dying?' My response is always the same. In my experience people are not usually afraid of dying. They are afraid; but not of dying. It is the arrogance of strength and health that presumes that people must be afraid of dying, but when it comes to it people rarely are. The fear surrounding death usually falls into the categories of fear of dying in pain and fear of leaving behind someone, or several people, that they love. So fear of death becomes fear of losing that which they love. When you can understand the difference, how you respond pastorally is very different.

There are two examples of dying I would like to share with you. The first one was Lucy, a girl of 21. She was the same age as my daughter at the time and an alcoholic. She had had many stays in hospital over the year and each time had been told by the doctors that unless she gave up drinking she would eventually die. Lucy knew the risks, but the system let her down. I originally came into contact with her through a referral from an aunt who lived in Cornwall, who had been to visit Lucy several times previously. Each time Lucy came out of hospital promising that she would not drink, but she was drinking again within days. Over the months when she was on the ward I learnt that Lucy's father had walked out on the family when she was two, and she and her mum were very close. When Lucy was 18 her mum died of cancer and it had hit Lucy hard. Since then she had ceased to feel that anyone loved her and she felt she was not able to love anyone for fear they would also leave her. She had found solace in the bottle and, like a lot of alcoholics, any friends that she did have slowly disappeared from her life. When you are slowly dying from liver poisoning it is a very horrible, unpleasant death. There can be a lot of sickness and bloating. Your skin and eyes become yellow, your hair becomes lank. I visited her on many occasions and was amazed at what a nice girl she was. She was very polite and always had lovely manners even when she was extremely poorly. This hit me because like everyone else I have prejudices regarding certain people. Even though I make every effort not to judge people, I find my subconscious has judged someone long before my conscious self has intervened and righted it.

Lucy would sit in bed being sick into a bowl and I would perch on the bed behind her, rubbing her back while she was throwing up. On my last visit she was in a dreadful state, and between retches she was apologizing to me for being sick; for returning to hospital and for letting everyone down. I have never felt so completely helpless, or that a situation was so hopeless. I did not know this particular visit would be my last one, of course. We had been through the rounds of throwing up, but this time she did not rally. She was lying facing the window and I was rubbing her back talking to her when the doctor appeared in the doorway and shook his head at me. I will never forget it. We were in a side room off the ward. I sat on the bed, put my arms around her and wept my heart out. When I looked down she had died in my arms. With all the noises of the ward bustling outside, she had simply slipped away. I was completely unprepared for it and it was the first time someone had actually died in my arms, but I thank God that I was there at that moment and she did not die alone. She was not afraid of dying; in fact I think she welcomed it. Lucy was afraid of living. I have never forgotten Lucy, and because of her I tell my own daughter every day that I love her and I thank God that we have each other to love.

The second example was baby Henry, who had been born at 24 weeks. Now remember that in termination terms a baby with medical issues can be aborted up to 24 weeks. I say this because before entering onto a neonatal ward it is important to have thought through the ethical issues surrounding termination and assisted living. The youngest baby I have had contact with was 21 weeks. It is difficult to watch a tiny little baby fighting for its life when you realize that that same baby could have been elected to be terminated. As in the previous example, we need to acknowledge our own feelings. Denying how you feel is not the same as processing your thoughts and feelings and finding a pastoral path that is acceptable to patients but does not compromise your integrity. The way I cope with this is to acknowledge that each case and situation is different and complex. It is not my place to judge anyone but to support them pastorally in the decision that they make. This is very difficult and it is the subject I believe that most divides chaplains. I think it is much better to acknowledge if this is a challenge to your theology and talk it through with your colleagues to make sure that patients get the best possible support that is available to them in their moment of need. It is not a sign of weakness but indicates that you have thought prayerfully and carefully considered the situation, and that you realize the decision you make will not be an easy one.

On a neonatal unit there are usually two reasons for calling in a chaplain as an emergency. The first is to baptize a baby that is not expected to live, and the second is when the doctors have decided to withdraw treatment. The latter was the case with Henry. His parents were not religious, which is often the case with young parents, but when they had been told what Henry's fate was, having been offered a chaplain they accepted. After I had arrived and spent some time with the parents, and the rest of the family had been called in, the nurses brought Henry into the family room, which is a room decorated as a nursery. A Moses basket was in the corner of the room and there was also a comfortable settee. Henry was finally free of the tubes and masks that had been his constant companion since birth, and he was given to Mum and Dad. They had 15 minutes with him. Both Mum and Dad held him, but the rest of the family stood quietly in the corner. I said some prayers for him and then he slipped away. After some time I asked Mum if she would like her mum to hold her grandson. The family were hesitant at first, but then slowly they held him and talked to him. This I have found helps in the grieving process. Years ago babies like Henry would not have stood a chance and his death would have been handled far less sensitively, but by encouraging those who love the parents to be part of this intense grieving process then whatever comes in the future they will have this shared experience. They will have someone else that knew Henry to talk to, who knows what happened that night when all that they had hoped for was snatched away from them. This is really hard on everyone including the person giving the pastoral care: never underestimate the effect it will have on you.

Finding out what makes someone afraid is the first step to helping them. I couldn't help Lucy, but she was afraid of facing a world alone, not of dying. Encouraging families to make peace, to talk about what's on their minds, facilitating discussions and trying to answer questions is a really important aspect of our role. With Henry's parents they were most afraid that Henry was alone somewhere. I was able to draw on the resurrection and the promise of eternal life to reassure them of my belief that he was going straight into the arms of Christ and would never be alone. I also assured them of my belief that they would one day be reunited with him.

What actually happens when someone dies

This section has been difficult to write and I would guess it is hard to read, but if you want to support someone who is bereaved it is important that you acquaint yourselves with the facts about death. This will make you a more efficient communicator and competent pastoral support.

The first time I came into contact with a dead body was many years ago when I was on a placement in theological college. The minister who was supervising me dropped me one day at the funeral directors. I spent the morning preparing a person for embalmment. A bit morbid, but I have looked back many times and thought that was probably one of the most useful things I did at college. In a safe environment it got all the doubts, fears and unexpected noises and facial expressions out of the way. As a minister you are often expected to go and sit with someone that has died at home. You do not want to let yourself down with an unexpected reaction so if you can go and do some preparation beforehand it is well worth it.

Unfortunately death is not like *Casualty* where patients are in a dimly lit, quiet side room, looking very peaceful, saying their final words of wisdom to a family around their bed before slipping peacefully away. What I am going to write next is not easy, but in this book I am giving an honest account of the role of chaplains, clergy and volunteers so you need to know that death is not always a pleasant event.

On one occasion I visited a man who was in the final stages of life. It was a routine visit for me and I was not expecting anything unusual. After talking to his wife and daughter, who were sitting there, I approached the bed. I started saying some prayers when suddenly he convulsed and blood poured out of his mouth and covered him. The nurse who was standing opposite me looked panicked. The family did not see anything as they were sitting down praying with me, so I continued the prayers without faltering, indicating to the nurse to quickly clear him up with my facial expression and hands. They were the longest prayers I have ever done, covering for her so that they did not see what actually looked like a scene from a horror movie. The family were none the wiser, the nurse, although young, was excellent, and by the time I had finished he was looking clean and peaceful again.

Your face must not betray you. In the neonatal unit, for example, babies often die because of an abnormality. I have seen some terrible disfigurements. I always ask if I can hold the baby and kiss the top of its head. Remember that this is someone's precious baby. Sometimes you do not know what you will see when you look in the cot. Practise your facial expressions; it is important.

One such baby was 'Angel'. I picked up the baby as I usually do, only for blood to come out of her eyes and mouth. The top of her head had caved in. The mum lifted her little hat off to show me. You can never presume what will happen in an encounter: be prepared for the worst. The wrong reaction will likely have a lasting effect on the family that they may never recover from.

When someone dies in hospital they are not usually kept on the ward for more than a few hours. If you are called to a situation it is important that you get there within that time if you are required to say prayers. After this the body is moved to the mortuary. There are special circumstances for Muslim and Jewish patients, who are required by religious law to bury their bodies within 24 hours wherever possible. It can be most distressing for patients who want to see their loved ones over the weekend when the mortuary is possibly shut and there is no or limited access available to them. This requires sensitive pastoral support.

Conclusion

Some Christians would say that death and the crucifixion is at the heart of our Christian faith. I wear a cross round my neck, which is very precious to me. It was chosen because it has flowers inscribed upon the cross to remind me not of death but of what came next: the resurrection, new life, new hope. There can be no resurrection without the pain and suffering of death. That is expressed in many forms in our world today. Nature has its own cycle of birth, death and rebirth, with the turning of the seasons. Christ had a bloody and painful death, which we are told was so that all people (you and me) could be free of the burden of guilt and sin. What I see in the gospel is that one person sacrificed himself so that we could have a chance at being better, but the resurrection confirms for us that there is so much more waiting for us following the inevitability of death. How we die is important. To be at peace with ourselves and our loved ones is priceless. To die with dignity and without suffering is the real gift of the cross, but it is just the beginning. It is in the resurrection that we can reassure people that heaven exists, that God waits for us and that it will be free of the burdens of this world.

In this chapter we have looked in depth at the concept of the Liverpool Care Pathway and the practical implications that has on patient experience. We have explored the importance of having difficult conversations with our families and friends and how to bring death into our everyday lives. We have examined the fears surrounding dying and how to support families pastorally through those difficult hours. We have had an honest account of what can actually happen physically and institutionally when a patient dies. In conclusion we have looked at some theological perspectives on the issues on death and resurrection.

Key Points

- The LCP was introduced to aid people in the process of death. If it is removed something will replace it. It is designed to make sure that spiritual needs are addressed, that a patient's preferred place of death is respected where possible and that invasive, unnecessary treatment is avoided. It also enables the difficult conversations that allow families to prepare for letting go to be facilitated. While there have been problems with the LCP, the concept is sound and what it evolves into should, if possible, be supported.

- Try to encourage people to embrace death as part of life, to have difficult conversations before it becomes too painful – that is, when you are young and your life is not nearing its end. So many families cope better when those conversations have already been had; it releases families from the conflict and guilt of not being sure what their loved one would have wanted.

- Trying to get behind what is causing someone to be fearful and working on ways in which you can bring some peace to the situation are important aspects of our role. It is rare that people are actually afraid of dying in the end, when death is close. Find out what their fears are.

- Real death is very rarely like *Casualty*. The reality of death can be hard and brutal. Equip yourself with as much preparation as you can. The wrong reaction can have devastating effects on a family or those supporting the patient.

9

The challenge of mental health

Introduction

In this chapter I will give a brief overview of the different types of support that patients or service-users who are affected by a mental illness may require. This is by no means a full and comprehensive list. There are many different ways in which pastoral and spiritual support can be provided. First, we will look at the practical ways in which, as care-givers, we can support those patients who have dementia. We will then look at the way in which we can support people in the community, including in our own churches, who have a mental illness. Finally, the challenges that may arise when supporting people in secure units with mental-health issues will be analysed, with theological reflections interwoven through the chapter.

Practical coping strategies for visiting patients with dementia

When considering how best to support patients with dementia it is important to get a good understanding of the term. Dementia is used when describing a range of different brain disorders. Alzheimer's disease is reported as the most common type of dementia, affecting around 62 per cent of those diagnosed. There are other types of dementia, including vascular dementia, which affects around 17 per cent of those diagnosed, and mixed dementia, affecting around 10 per cent of those diagnosed, according to the Alzheimer's Association. It is a sad fact that there are currently 800,000 people reported to have dementia in the UK with a predicted forecast of over 1 million by 2021. It is estimated that this will rise to 1.7 million by 2050. One in three people will die with dementia. Currently 80 per cent of those people being cared for in care homes have dementia or severe memory conditions, according to the Alzheimer's Association.

Caring for someone with dementia can often be a demanding and challenging job. Whether that person is caring at home, in the community or whether the person they love has moved either on a temporary basis or permanently into residential care can provide many difficult and distressing situations. There can be stressful decisions that need to be made. There are ways in which we can offer practical as well as spiritual support to both the carer and the person being cared for. I will look at the two groups separately as their needs are different. First, I will look at how to support the person who has dementia.

The patient or service-user with dementia

When a person first finds that they are suffering with dementia it can be a slow and painful process. Often it begins with memory loss – easily laughed off within the confines of a loving relationship, 'the problems of old age'. It can manifest itself with lost car keys, difficulty remembering familiar routes when you are out and about, the name that slips your mind. We are all victim to this kind of memory loss and the older you get the more it seems to be happening. It is actually quite a frightening stage, both for the person who is losing their memory and those around them. Many different emotions and behaviours are displayed including denial and secrecy. Sometimes, partners will 'cover up' for their loved one, making allowances, not wanting to face the reality of the situation. Other times, partners will seek help from family members, only to be ignored as they go into denial and cannot cope with reliable Mum or Dad showing weakness and vulnerability. Sometimes those suffering will get very angry, even aggressive, and take it out on those close to them, which can bring about shame and therefore a reluctance to admit what exactly is happening. There are many different scenarios and I think I have experienced nearly all of them during my time in ministry. They are difficult to address as you are never quite sure of the scenario that you are facing. There are, however, some simple practical steps that you can undertake to help the person with dementia.

Early stages of dementia

Understanding and respecting the person's autonomy is crucial in all aspects of healthcare work but never more so than with the onset of dementia. There cannot be a single person in this country who has failed to see the awful news stories and documentaries surrounding the level of acceptable care in care homes. That I am sure is the first and most terrifying thought as someone comes to realize that they may have onset dementia, wondering what is going to be their fate. Therefore a safe, honest listening ear is a simple yet effective part of your tool box. If you are privileged enough for someone to confide in you that they are worried about memory loss, then try not to do what those who love them will probably do. In a very calm way use the communication skills tools discussed in Chapter 4. Listen intently, do not belittle or ignore their concerns and do not over-reassure. You cannot say to someone, 'Oh, I'm sure it's nothing to worry about,' because clearly it is a concern for the conversation to be taking place. This is the most tempting of responses because it will almost certainly bring a very short period of relief. However, you may just be putting off the inevitable and in doing so have lost valuable time in beginning to establish a trusting, honest relationship. The person needs to feel listened to, valued and not judged. Your role here is unique. As you are not a clinician, you cannot prescribe, suggest a care home or package or ultimately section them, as a doctor or other clinician could do. It is vital to acknowledge your exclusive role: you cannot 'do' anything to this person, therefore you are a safe person to talk to. The worst thing that you can do is ignore them and refuse to take their concerns seriously. Done correctly, it can be an incredibly rewarding and helpful role. So if someone talks to you, use your skills of communication and help them discover the pathway that they want to take, in their own time.

It might be that you are asked to be present during a conversation with family and loved ones. Here you can use facilitation skills to help make sure that everyone gets a chance to speak, to contribute to the conversation and be listened to and respected. It might be that you are asked to accompany the person to a doctor's appointment, if they feel that is the next step for them. The offer of a lift without the worry about parking is really helpful. You do not necessarily need to enter into the intimacy of the consultation process. A friendly face greeting them in the waiting room can go a long way to relieving someone's stress and worry. One of the most effective practical ways you can help is in your total acceptance of them when they have been brave enough to talk to you about their dementia. Remember that most people fear the responses that the society they live in will make; derogatory remarks about mental health are sadly all too common. Make sure that once someone has confided in you, you carry on your relationship with them as normal. Try not to back away, do not be fearful of what to say and end up ignoring them; this is exactly what they are worried about. The onset of established dementia can take up to seven years. If someone confides in you that they are starting to lose their memory or get a bit confused and need help, this does not mean they will change overnight. You have nothing to fear from spending time with them.

Progressive dementia

When dementia has progressed there may be several routes for families to consider. The person may be cared for at home by a loved one or team of carers. They may attend 'day centres', have occasional respite or be permanently living in a care home. It is often difficult for families when visiting their loved ones at this stage and there are ways in which you can help. It is particularly difficult at this stage when the person ceases to recognize those around them and cannot have a conversation with their loved ones. A practical way in which you can help is to arrange to go into a facility and take in an activity. My activity is singing. I have always loved music and at times of great difficulty in my life have found it to be both a healer and an inspirer. I go into the community hospitals and other establishments with my CD player with favourite hymns. When I arrive there the room often looks quite a grim scene. There are many people with dementia sitting round the room, some asleep, some shouting out in fear, some continuously asking for relatives or when they can go home. This work is not for the faint-hearted and do not think it will not break your heart many times over, because it will. However, when I start playing the first hymn, usually 'All things bright and beautiful', the room slowly starts to wake from the land of forgotten dreams and shattered memories. The wall dividing them from this world is torn in two. The patients start singing the familiar words to songs learnt long ago, captured in their memories waiting for the key to release them again. I challenge anyone not to shed a tear when the swell of music and singing of old songs resonates round a small lounge. These patients are often forgotten by the busy world outside, or worse, discarded by a society whose values are not in line with God's. I often wonder at God watching this moment. What does he/she think when his/her sheep are returned to the field, safe once more, even if only for just a short while before returning to their lost world again.

It is at times like this that we must remember the people that care for these lost souls. I was taking one of the singing sessions on a Thursday morning when I noticed a new lady. She was very large, dressed in manly clothes and with cropped short hair – a very distinct look as against the other patients of the hospital. Her name was Margaret and she was clearly quite distressed. When you are dealing with someone with dementia the first rule is to try not to aggravate them as they can get very stressed and upset. Margaret was looking for her friend and thought that one of the other ladies in the room was the friend she had been searching for. The staff were trying to distract her away from this lady, and several of the other residents were being quite unkind about her appearance. They were shouting out, asking loudly if she was a man or a woman, and why she dressed like a man. Margaret did not understand why they were shouting at her and why she could not sit beside her 'friend' and hold her hand. This could have been an innocent act that she would have done at home in her life before dementia. It reminds me of the harshness of this world in which we live and that discrimination and unkindness can be found in every corner, even given out by people who themselves are wounded soldiers. Reaching out and being able to understand people is an important role in our profession, with a non-judgemental approach.

Carers often feel abandoned when a loved one goes into residential care, or feel that the focus is on the patient or service-user and they have become invisible. The carer needs support that will give them a level of visibility and let them know that someone cares. Email support is a popular support-mechanism, particularly for those just getting to grips with information technology or younger carers. There seems to be a popular trend towards anonymity and people feel more able to express themselves if it is not face to face. One-to-one support can also be needed. A home visit, sharing a cup of tea with someone and asking about them, as well as mediating in case conferences when relationships with staff are becoming fraught or they feel not listened to are all valuable ways to support people.

I asked the staff to give my card to Margaret's 'friend' when she next came in and I received a call shortly afterwards. I went to see Joan at home, a delightful lady in her 70s. She told me of the life that she and Margaret had shared together. They had been partners for 50 years and in that time had seen much discrimination and the ugliness of human nature. Joan was a forgiving lady with a round, smiley face. She looked like someone's grandma. She had lots of pictures of nieces and nephews, graduation pictures and other family occasions. It was obvious that despite plotting a difficult life-course, the two had shared a lifetime of happiness and been the bedrock of their extended family. I asked what I could do to help. Joan was upset that Margaret was experiencing discrimination and unkindness from the other patients. She had been sent there for rehabilitation following an operation and they had realized that she had dementia; a fact that, Joan told me, she had been carefully hiding for several years. They were private people and did not want to have interference from the authorities. When Joan had gone to visit Margaret and said she was her 'friend', the staff had been dismissive of her and had not included her in the care planning. The staff had asked to speak to her 'family', although Margaret had no 'blood family'. I was able to persuade Joan to let me talk to the staff and advise them of the true nature of their relationship, which I did. Once the staff were aware that Joan was in fact Margaret's partner and selected next of kin, her relationship with the staff improved. There was now an understanding of Margaret's behaviour which they managed far better knowing what her situation was, and the acts of discrimination were handled sensitively and with compassion. I accompanied Joan to the case conference and supported her while she made the application to have the appropriate support package put in place so that Margaret could come home. Having not wanted to visit Margaret, Joan became more confident and did visit. She came to a singing session before Margaret's discharge and the two of them joined in singing together. I still see both of them every month at home and it remains one of the highlights of my month.

Tackling discrimination is for me an important aspect of my role. No one human being should oppress, discriminate against or make judgements on another human being; yet of course they do. I often think of the story of the Good Samaritan and what that says for us as people of faith in the world today. In its simplest form there are many people who we think perhaps get what they deserve, should be left on the roadside, are just bad, but the call to all Christians is to cross over the road of hatred, injustice and malevolence, reaching out to those in need; not seeing them as the world sees them, not judging them as current society judges them but seeing them through the eyes of God. All people are the children of God, sometimes lost and afraid, always needing love and support.

Ethical dilemmas of the secure units

In my current post I visit all types of secure units from high to low security. These are for people with complex and challenging mental-health issues that are a danger to themselves or society. Some of these service-users are detained by Her Majesty's Pleasure; some are too unwell to be sentenced. There is of course a great deal of training on personal safety, and measures are put in place to help you stay safe when you enter one of these facilities. I want to give the potential chaplain, volunteer or priest some idea of the challenges to be faced when working in this environment.

What to expect

When entering a secure unit it is likely you will be photographed, and mobile phones, keys and ID will be removed from you and locked away so that you cannot reach them. You will be given an alarm that can be activated if you feel you are under threat. If you press this alarm, staff will arrive from all directions within seconds to aid you. They will restrain the person and remove them from you, if you are being attacked, with reasonable force. They are trained to do this. It can, however, be very frightening, even just hearing an alarm go off. If one does go off when you are visiting and it is not yours, stay where you are and staff will return. Do not try to follow or offer help, but keep well back. It is not your job to help. You should receive training in how to defend yourself, but do not try to rescue someone else; help will arrive within a very short time. If you are in a corridor keep your back to the wall and body tucked in so that staff can run past you; do not speak or distract them in any way. Someone else's life is at risk.

When seeing someone with complex needs always seek the advice of the staff member. Never give any items to the service-user, and always let the staff member know what you are doing. I was called to a girl called Angela, who was suffering through a bereavement. I said some prayers and we talked. At the end she asked me if I could give her a copy of one of the prayers she found most helpful, which I gladly agreed to. I told the staff member on my way out and she said 'Sorry, no'; that particular girl used paper to block her orifices in suicide attempts. Do not assume you have 'worked out' someone in one of these units; I am always shocked at my own ability to get people wrong.

I and my colleagues go into these units to give services, which include communion. I also give talks, Bible study and praise and fellowship (singing) in some units. This is one of the few occasions when men and women are allowed to be in the same room. The staff do keep them separate but all sorts of high jinks can go on around you. Keep your eyes and ears open. Never turn your back and never allow yourself to be alone with someone. People are not placed in high secure units for no good reason. Do not be naive, or it will be at your peril. I do not wish to frighten you, but I do want you to take your personal safety seriously.

Never give away personal information that can identify you to an area, person or place. Learn to not divulge answers to questions like, 'Are you married?' 'Do you have children?' 'Do you live near here?' The more identifiable information you give out, the more at risk your personal safety is. Having said all that, I really enjoy this aspect of my work. Obviously do not agree to give notes, pass on messages or bring anything in for anyone, despite how reasonable and innocent it may seem. One image that comes into my mind is the Samaritan woman at the well. In the Gospels we see her speaking to Christ and the way in which he just understood her, inside and out, knew her and accepted her. Jesus did not patronize, but called the woman into service, just as she was, not dependent on changing and being a better, different person. Jesus looked into her eyes, saw her soul and asked her for the living water, and she quenched his thirst. Many of the women in these units have scarred arms, legs and sometimes even necks from self-harming. They are hurting inside and out, yet sit together singing 'Kumbaya' with gusto while the world outside is battered by the elements, the rain lashing against the window and the hail smashing angrily on the hard cold slabs. It is moments like this that bring for me the gospel message of acceptance and love into reality. It reminds me that there is a place for all in the kingdom of God. You begin to realize that we have no idea at all of the wonder and magnificence of God's love in our life or his ability to transform and change us through grace alone.

Supporting patients and service-users in the community – in our churches

Mental-health challenges are very common, according to the charity MIND: one in four people in Britain suffers with a mental illness. These can be of varying severity according to diagnosis, including anxiety and depression, obsessive com- pulsive disorder, phobias, bipolar disorder (formerly known as manic depression), schizophrenia, personality disorders and eating disorders. You are not expected to know and understand all the nuances of the different types of mental illness, but be aware that if one in four of the population suffers from a men- tal illness then a large number of the people in your church, family and community may be battling with this illness in some form, maybe without knowing it themselves. One of the challenges people face is the stigma and discrimination, along with myths that run concurrently with diagnosis. Many people do not want to speak of their challenges out of fear of rejection or humiliation in the reaction of those around them. It is important to remember that someone who has a mental-health problem can recover from their illness and live a productive and fulfilling life. It is not a sign of weakness, it is the sign of an illness. As with any other illness, it can be treated and, with enough care and compassion, people can recover from it or learn to live with it and incorporate it into their lives.

Signs of being mentally unwell

Self-harming

There are various signs that indicate someone may be mentally unwell or becoming so. One is that someone may start to self-harm, particularly in the case of young people but not exclusively. It can be a way to express deep distress, a way of communicating what the person feels which they can't put into words. It has been described as an 'inner scream'. After someone has self-harmed they often feel some relief and perhaps able to cope with life again, for a while – although without the root problem being identified and addressed, it is unlikely that relief will be a long-term solution. If you notice that someone is covering their arms or other areas of their body, perhaps when it is warm weather and the clothing seems inappropriate, this may be a sign that they are self-harming and wishing to conceal it from those who care for them. Building a relationship of trust with this person is the way to support them, a relationship where they feel able to talk to you about what is happening to them. Try not to ask them to show you their arms; do not try to trick them into revealing their body parts. If you are going to help them it has to be on their terms. Wait until they are ready to tell you what is going on. Your reaction is important; try not to be shocked, angry, upset. This is not about you, it is about them. If you can, be open, accepting and let them lead the way. Sadly you are not going to be able to cure them, sort it out or change their behaviour. It is too serious for you to attempt that. Your role is to offer a listening, non-judgemental ear. You are the accompanier to clinical help, perhaps the mediator to parents or partners. You should not offer your opinions at this time. Plenty of people will have an opinion; therefore the challenge is to be simply alongside the person, being a loving friend. This could take months, but it is worth the investment of not rushing. If you get this right the recovery and solution will be far more effective. This person's pain is deep and complex; it needs specialist help.

One experience of self-harming I had was when I was called to attend to Sue. Sue was in a secure unit. She had burnt down her house when high on cocaine and alcohol. Sue could not remember the incident and although she accepted she had done it, had no recollection of the night. Sue had a son who had been taken into care and she was a regular self-harmer. It was our ritual to meet weekly. Sue could not read and so each week I took in a Gospel reading in large print and I was teaching her to read through the Gospel stories: it was an experience of Christ reaching out from those stories in an incarnational way, presented to us in the moment, alongside us. Her inability to read seemed to be the root cause of her self-harming; as a child she had been abused, burnt with cigarettes and sexually abused with painful methods of punishment, which went on for years. Sue was told that she was ugly and useless, and she believed it. Being physically prevented from trying to learn to read contributed to her abusers' control of her and became a way to reinforce her lack of self-belief. When I came into contact with Sue, she honestly believed she was no use to herself or society. Addressing the reading issue was the beginning of Sue's taking control of her life and believing that she was someone important and had some purpose. To do that through the Gospel stories meant that as we read, we learnt and talked about Christ's acceptance of everyone. We talked about the sheep that was lost and not given up on; the way in which the woman who was brave enough to reach out and touch Christ's cloak was healed. We talked about how even Judas was forgiven and loved in all his sinfulness. This is not a story of happiness and recovery. Many times when I went into visit Sue, she would have wrecked her room and been relegated to blues (not being allowed to wear their own clothes for fear of self-harming). She was regularly on suicide watch and often had new flesh wounds. What was important was to let her set the pace. Sometimes I think she was testing me, wanting me almost to be disappointed in her for regressing, but I never was. I never let her see me flinch at the ugliness of the wounds, even when she cut her neck. I just picked up and started with her again from where she was at that moment. Sue's problems were too big for me to help with, or sort out, but I could give her something of myself. I gave my commitment not to give up on her, not to be disappointed in her, not to judge her and not to ask more of her than she could give. She in turn showed me her beauty within, just glimpses now and again, not permanently. I saw her inner pureness, and that life and experience had hardened and corrupted her, but through the grace of God we shared some intimate moments that brought glory to the surface and the hope that a new dawn might be realized one day.

Suicidal thoughts

Depression can affect people in many ways. Sometimes it is difficult to discern and would need a clinical diagnosis to define depression as opposed to what is deemed the 'normal' response to life's ups and downs. Bereavement, divorce, loss of job or family difficulties – all or any of these might bring about a period of 'the blues', 'trouble with nerves' or a description of being 'a bit low': some of the many ways the different generations describe depression. This is not perhaps clinical depression but still needs support and encouragement. Often people may say they need to 'snap out of it' or 'pull themselves together'. Please do not be one of those well-meaning people.

If someone could snap out of it they would. No one likes feeling lost, lonely, vulnerable or lacking in hope. Do something practical instead of telling someone what they should do. Offer a listening ear, either formally or over a coffee, and really listen to them. Offer to 'do' something with them. Motivation can be a problem and they find it hard to get themselves together on their own. Invite them to the walking group, friendship circle or choir, for example, and 'carry' them along. Try not to notice if they are not very chatty. Just act normally around them without making them feel self-conscious. Eventually they will come round and start participating again. What they do not need is continuous questioning about whether they are all right or, worse, being ignored because they make you feel uncomfortable.

If someone reveals to you that they have suicidal tendencies, that is one occasion that overrides the confidential clause. If you find out that someone is considering harming themselves or another person, you have a responsibility to inform someone in authority what you have been told. Even if someone wants to tell you a 'secret', you must give a proviso that you will keep their confidence as long as what they tell you does not indicate that they are likely to harm themselves or another person. You can guide the person to confidential listening lines such as the Samaritans and ChildLine. But under no circumstances must you keep this type of information to yourself out of a misguided concern for confidentiality.

It is a sad fact that some people do commit suicide, and that most of those who intend to commit suicide, however much help and support they are given, if they want to do it enough will find a way. I have taken the funerals of six suicide victims over the years. Each one was extremely sad. One young man left a young wife and two children. He had suffered with manic depression; it tore the family apart, with his parents blaming his wife and his wife blaming his parents. No one, of course, was to blame. He had an illness that could not be managed or controlled and ultimately he could not cope with it any longer. There are so many victims in suicide cases. It means a life sentence for those left behind. Your role is to comfort the bereaved with reassurance that the God we worship loves and accepts all into his kingdom; one of people's biggest fears lies in the theology that sends the suicide soul to damnation. I believe my loving God holds all his people in his arms, especially the lost and the broken. They are the ones that Jesus came to save. They surely will have a place in heaven.

Panic attacks

People who have panic attacks have probably the most common form of mental illness and in some ways are the most easily supported. One in ten people experience panic attacks at some level, varying in degrees of intensity. Some people have recurring and regular panic attacks, sometimes seemingly for no recognizable reason, though usually brought on by anxiety. Anxiety is a feeling of unease. It can range from mild to severe, and can include feelings of worry or fear. Several different conditions can cause anxiety. Phobia, for example, is an extreme or irrational fear of an animal, object, place or situation. General anxiety disorder is a long-term condition that causes anxiety in an excessive way and also can cause worry that may relate to particular situations. In post-traumatic stress disorder psychological and physical symptoms are experienced which can be caused by frightening or distressing events.

A panic attack occurs when your body experiences a rush of intense psychological and physical symptoms. The person may feel frightened and anxious combined with physical symptoms such as trembling, sweating, nausea and palpitations. A panic attack itself will not harm the person. It would not normally require admittance to hospital, for example. If you are with someone who has a panic attack there are some simple things you can do to help them through the initial phase. First, do not try to move them. An attack can last for up to an hour, so just stay with them through it – there is no quick fix. Help them to focus on something visible that is not threatening. Tell the person what you are doing. Do not try to distract them. Say, 'It will help you to focus on something', or 'I'm going to tell you a story and I want you to listen to it.' Look at or watch something together – children playing, a cricket match, whatever is near to you. Try to encourage them not to breathe too quickly, as this can make the attack worse. Breathe slowly together. Breathing is something to focus on that is not threatening. If the person is panicking about dark thoughts such as death, dying, illness or violence, try talking them through some basic meditation techniques, such as 'Imagine you are by the river . . .', then describe a beautiful non-threatening place. Try to get the person to relax. Do not try to talk them out of it. Accept it is happening but reassure them that this will pass if they focus, breathe and imagine calm things. When the attack has passed, encourage the person to seek professional help with their anxiety while reassuring them that what they have experienced is fairly common and there is nothing to be embarrassed or feel ashamed about. Talking about mental-health issues helps to break down barriers and encourages people to be honest about their concerns and worries and to seek help when they need it.

Mental health and the Bible have a tenuous relationship. There are many examples, the most easily recognized being the Gerasene Demonic, where Jesus ceremoniously exorcized the evil spirit from a man and sent the demons, of which there were many, into a herd of swine. For the animal lovers among us, it's a challenging story on that level alone. Clearly in Jesus' time, people with severe mental-health issues were supposed to be possessed by the devil. Over 2,000 years later, with the intervention of medical knowledge, compassion and understanding, we now know that some of those behaviours were a clear sign of what we understand today to be mental-health illness. These stories are often misused by preachers and the uneducated among us, spreading fear and discord among people. The story of the healing of the demonic is a story of healing, of Christ's willingness to go where others feared. He reached out and healed the man of all that harmed him. If we allow the focus to be on possession we are missing the point of Christ's ministry.

Christ came for all people, those who were ill, those who were broken, those who needed to find themselves, and reached out to them and touched them. He touched them far deeper than curing an illness, but touched them deep within their souls and transformed them. That is the story of the Gospels.

Conclusion

In this chapter we have looked at an overview of mental illness. We have seen how it affects patients and service-users, their carers and families, and how to support all those affected, including those people who may have mild mental illness within our own families and church communities. We have identified good practice within a range of institutions including secure units, and reflected theologically on several examples of inclusion and healing from the Gospel stories.

Key Points

- Be aware that currently one in three people will die with dementia. Mental health will affect you, your family or church community in some way. This is not something that will go away.
- Fear is the biggest barrier to people seeking help. Often families will cover up for loved ones. Try not to belittle worries, ignore concerns or normalize fears.
- For progressive dementia – try activities like singing, taking communion, saying the Lord's Prayer. Familiar words or activities help provide distraction and unlock lost memories.
- For the carer – being a carer can be really isolating. Help them with practical tasks, mediation on wards and general caring for them, as the attention often is on the patient.

- Signs of mental illness – only a selection of examples have been provided here. If someone confides to you suicidal tendencies or a desire to harm others, that completely overrides any confidence clause. You must seek help and advice immediately.

- In secure units – work with the service-user's truth and the future not the past. Keep safe, never presume you understand the full situation, and take advice from staff and colleagues.

Sustaining oneself in the face of suffering

Introduction

In this chapter we will look how as professionals or volunteers we sustain ourselves in the face of suffering. We will cover what we mean by 'good practice'. We will look at the use of humour in difficult situations and how to leave our pain at the foot of the cross. We will assess theological perspectives on personal sacrifice and personal sustenance, identifying what that means for us in today's world. First we will look at the area of good practice.

Good practice

The idea and concept of good practice in medical terms is developed and published by the General Medical Council (GMC). The GMC covers four domains of service provision: knowledge, skills and performance; safety and quality; communication, partnership and teamwork; and maintaining trust. While this guidance is targeted at doctors, the standards set by the GMC have a lot to teach us as healthcare professionals. They set a benchmark which I think is worth measuring ourselves against, and which can benefit how we look after and sustain ourselves through this complex ministry when we face so much suffering.

Knowledge

The GMC guidelines state that you, as a healthcare professional, should be competent in all areas of your work and keep your professional knowledge up to date. I have recently completed a Masters in Palliative Care and cannot express how much benefit this has given me in my practice. I come from a non-clinical background and I have learnt so much working alongside clinicians and have come to understand and talk the NHS talk. It stretched me beyond my imagination. I am not suggesting that everyone should need or want to complete further academic study, but I would encourage you to take what opportunities for extra study or training are made available to you. It is difficult when staff levels have been cut to a minimum and perhaps, like me, you will only be able to pursue extra training in your own time. The benefit to my practice, however, has without doubt superseded any obstacles that training raised for me. It also instils in you the discipline of keeping abreast of current literature and updating your knowledge base of guidelines relevant to your service area, which you may otherwise pass over. Part of the way to sustaining yourself is through knowledge.

Reflective practice

The GMC guidelines on safety and quality encourage regular reflection on personal practice. This is something that in theological college used to be our mantra: 'on personal reflection'; but thinking about what has happened in the day, looking back and perhaps evaluating how things could have been done more effectively, is an important lesson for us. However, when you are dealing with patients in hospital there are two issues to take into consideration. First, as expressed earlier in the book, some of the situations we face can be quite disturbing, and sharing that information with a loved one is not good practice. I learnt the hard way; very quickly you can become somewhat desensitized as to the impact that the number of deaths you are dealing with can have on those who are not in your situation. Talking about young people dying is quite a conversation stopper. Yet often you will come home and need to discuss or reflect on the day's events, as the day's events will have had an effect on you. You may find the following tip useful in sustaining you through reflection.

I'm a great fan of writing things down, so I find keeping a journal really helpful for personal reflection and getting out emotions. It is not for everyone but it is a good tool, just for your personal use. It can serve as a good reminder that however bad situations get, you do come through it, as well as recording the moments of joy you are privileged to witness. At the back of my journal I keep any thank-you notes I have been given. Things like this can help you remember why you are doing this job when things seem particularly difficult.

Supervision

I am an advocate for working with personal supervision. It is not currently a requirement of the role of priest or chaplain and there may not be a formal structure for volunteers to link in with. If you are a professional, you will find that someone who can act as a formal supervisor, spiritual director or listening friend is a most valuable resource. This person should be selected with great care. I was fortunate enough to have a colleague, and now friend, with whom I clicked. We shared a love of the role and understanding of the demands of the post, and those common experiences have bound us together. You cannot always find that in a team, for whatever reason. It needs to be someone with whom you feel safe, who understands the role and with whom you can be perfectly honest. Your sessions together should be regular rather than arranged on an ad hoc basis. This means that as well as using your journal if you have had a difficult week it can be reassuring to know that you have a session booked to reflect with someone who can sustain you professionally. Without this support the burden you carry could become too great and the chances of burn-out or depression may set in. For volunteers it is good to meet with the chaplain or the priest with pastoral charge on a regular basis to talk over any issues you have encountered. Try not to take things home with you; find some way to leave the patients in the hospital!

I remember interviewing a prospective volunteer for a community hospital in my charge. This lady was a very stoic woman, just into retirement, keen to fill her days with 'good works'. She had previously been a nurse and thought that visiting would be an excellent vocation for her. She was a straight-talking no-nonsense type and I had this very conversation with her about the need for support. When you are working in a community setting, seeing the chaplain regularly may not be a reality and often volunteering work can feel quite isolated. I remember she laughed when I suggested that she think through her support mechanisms and how she would emotionally cope with the complexities of chaplaincy visiting. She confidently informed me that after numerous years of nursing she thought she knew what she was doing. I relayed the support that was available to her should she need to access it and continued with the application process. Only a few months later she rang me in tears saying she wanted to resign her duties. There had been a lady on the ward she had got quite close to over several weeks who had suddenly died. It had completely thrown her and she was so upset she did not feel she wanted to carry on and risk going through that again.

A quiet community hospital with patients mainly undergoing rehabilitation could seem on the surface to be quite sedentary and lacking in the excitement of the acute setting. However, this is where relationships are really built up and lives and experiences shared. There is time to reflect on one's life, the joys and the sorrows, and time to contemplate the future and what it might bring. It is often within the confines of these relationships that the really difficult questions are asked, and they are usually asked of the person who has the time and energy and desire to listen. This is someone who sees beyond the little

ed properly and well, is something that will not affect you personally or drain you emotionally. If you give of yourself you have to be prepared to feel, and sometimes that will include sadness, as well as sharing the joy of seeing someone recover.

Teamwork

Working as a team in any setting is crucial. Being there to support one another has real value in your practice. When I worked in the acute setting, every morning we would start the day with the volunteers that were visiting that day a time of prayer. We were often joined by the other faith volunteers and chaplains, and we all shared in an important quiet time where we could still ourselves and pray for support for each other. This was also an opportunity to raise any concerns that were worrying us. We would ask for prayers if we knew we had a particularly difficult situation to address. In the community setting finding a time and place to get together can be a challenge due to lack of resources, but meeting as volunteers with the chaplain is a vital part of your combined ministry. Establishing relationships that nurture people's spirituality allows an honesty and understanding that mean that whenever a difficult situation arises you feel confident of the support structures that are in place so that you are only ever a phone call away from someone who understands and wants to listen to your concerns. Establishing a strong prayer link has been invaluable in the teams where I have worked. Often local churches will include the chaplaincy service provision in their prayers, and knowing that you and the work you are called to is being upheld in prayer can help to sustain you through the dark moments that you face. Never underestimate the power of prayer – after all we are taught where two or three are gathered in his name . . . This brings

128

me to the next section, which is the use of humour in a difficult situation.

Humour

Now as this is in the chapter about sustaining oneself rather than entertaining others, I will try to keep it in context. I am naturally a humorous person – a gift from my father who used humour at home to defuse any conflict, and I do this humour well. If humour doesn't come naturally to you – I don't think humour is something that you can learn – what you can do is understand the use of it in context, which may give you a greater insight into what you are observing around you. There are some key elements to understanding humour.

Relief theory

Relief theory states that the use of humour releases psychological tension, and in hospitals there is plenty of that: think Patch Adams, the founder of the Gesundheit Institute, who explored the benefits of laughter and fun, as well as other interventions with healing. Humour is not always appropriate and it can be used to intimidate and belittle people, so it needs to be used with care. As I say, I came from a household where my dad dealt with all tension with humour. It was never used to belittle anyone or with the objective of creating superiority complexes. Perhaps I was just lucky. Some groups of professionals have their own type of humour. Funeral directors are one. I have had some great laughs with funeral directors over the years, mainly because some of the situations I have been in have been so dreadful. If you did not laugh you'd break down. There was the time we could not get the coffin through the door and I was ad-libbing to the congregation while they were in the background turning the coffin 90 degrees to try to wedge it through the very narrow doorway. I was desperately trying to make sure the family were completely unaware that anything was wrong. Another time I had to expand the service because they had forgotten the lowering ropes to the grave. The men had to run back to the office while I said extemporary prayers for an extra 15 minutes until they arrived back. On one occasion they had brought the wrong coffin and I had to start the service while they took it back for the right one. I had to somehow blend it into the service: what else can you do but smile and carry on.

Taking yourself too seriously

In the Church, but in life as well, we can be in danger of taking ourselves too seriously. It is good to remember that we have a servant ministry and to keep our opinion of ourselves in perspective. The problem is that parishioners can have an inflated opinion of you. It is not *you* personally, it is the role. How many times will you hear, 'You cannot swear, drink, have political views, and such like. You are a vicar,' or 'Can I say that to someone of the cloth?' or even 'Can you do that as a Christian?', which I have never really understood. Keeping your feet on the ground is a real asset for self-sustenance. I have a large family round me and they have never let me be anything but myself, and most of my friends are from before pre-ordination training. I very rarely let anyone into my inner friendship circle who is impressed that I am a cleric. If you are able to laugh at yourself you will be far less hard on yourself in times of crisis. You may be thinking, 'I do not want to be soft on myself, I want to be tougher and get more professional and efficient.' I have found that it is in my mistakes that I am reminded of my humanity. It is in the tears I shed that I am reminded of my weakness. It is in the joys that I am reminded of the hope I can bring. I do not want to stop feeling vulnerable and weak because it is in that weakness that I believe God works the best in me and through me. This leads me on to how to leave the suffering of others, which you have taken upon yourself to ease their pain, at the foot of the cross, and in doing so sustain yourself.

At the foot of the cross

In earlier chapters I briefly looked at the emotional impact that the situations you may find yourself dealing with may have on your own wellbeing. At the heart of our Christian faith we are reminded that there is a crucifixion, a sacrificial offering by Christ himself to take away the sins of the world for us. You may or may not understand this well-used terminology, but for me the crucifixion, at its most basic, tells me that Christ went in my stead, died for me, for my failings, so that I could have life, new life. What that really means in reality for me is that when things are at their bleakest there is a place where I can go and be, in my vulnerability, completely honest. Then I can leave all the pain, suffering, anger and questions – which enables my own sustenance on the journey – at the foot of the cross.

The practical way for doing this is for me is to go to a chapel or church and spend some time in prayer. In that time of prayer I lift the concerns I have and find a way to leave them, whatever the challenges are. Sometimes situations really get inside you; you take people home with you mentally and they enter the innermost, intimate places of your soul and you hold them in your dreams. You are human, a living, loving human being, not a robot, and this *will* happen to you. Somehow you need to acknowledge this and deal with it in a way that is helpful to you.

I have a prayer buddy. She is my best friend and although I do not usually share the details of the person, I can say to her, 'I have brought someone home with me,' and she will know what I mean. I tell her the name of the person that is on my mind and we pray together. I am praying for the person and she prays for me to be at peace about them, accepting that I may not be able to help or make right the situation, and prays for strength for me to carry on my role. When I am angry, for example when a child dies or is suffering, I go through a practical ritual. I write down all my thoughts and frustrations. I have a place at the top of the garden with a little cross and some stones, unnoticed to the untrained eye. I keep a little silver bucket there. I place the paper in there and set it alight before the cross and when it is ash I tip it at the foot of the cross, say a prayer and walk away. Usually I leave all the pain there and I realize what a great sacrifice Christ made for me; the burden is lifted and I can continue on my journey of love. We cannot love those we need to love if our emotions are burdened with pain, grief and guilt. Leave all those negative emotions with Christ and free yourself for the task that you have been given, to LOVE.

Sometimes to sustain your emotional and mental wellbeing you need to challenge the authorities or speak out against something that you know to be wrong. The GMC advocate the taking of prompt action if you think a patient's safety, dignity or comfort is or may be seriously compromised while maintaining confidentiality. In light of the Francis Report it becomes even more vital that the routes to whistle-blowing are safely established, both for staff and for you. One of the roles of the chaplain is to sometimes challenge the institutional authorities within the healthcare environment they work in, as they are both patient and staff advocate. It is also important for you to have the relationships in place within your team to be able to confide in colleagues and line managers, to be able to assess the next step to take in the journey if you feel that patients' care, dignity and welfare are at risk.

Communication, partnership and teamwork are highlighted by the GMC as valuable support mechanisms in a healthcare environment. At the beginning of the job, or role, talk to your loved ones, partner and family, those you spend your evenings with and share your meal with. Explain the complexities that you might face in any one day and agree that you will not share those experiences over the table and upset everyone, and they in turn will accept if you say, 'It's been a bad day today,' and give you the space you need to process your thoughts and feelings. If you do not, and this is where I learnt the hard way, you will spoil what should be valuable family time with sadness and guilt. Remember that while you have been at it all day your family have also been doing things: life, school, shopping, having fun hopefully, or coping with the trauma of loves, lives and relationships as they experience it. Telling them of sadness when they are not prepared for it either brings about guilt in them or just spreads the sadness around. If you live alone, having a telephone support mechanism so you can talk to someone who knows what you are doing is really helpful. If they are happy for you to contact them any time if you have had a difficult encounter or just need to talk (being careful of confidentiality), having a chat until you feel a bit better can make all the difference.

Conclusion

Throughout this chapter, as we have reflected on how to sustain ourselves through this very demanding yet rewarding role of being called to care for others, overwhelmingly I have realized that the role we undertake is not a solo role. When the Gospels first pick up Jesus' journey, we see him collecting together his disciples. Often when preaching we reflect on the rugged rawness of his choice: big uneducated fishermen, a tax collector, doctor, theologian, to name a few. Jesus chose a cross-section of the community, all human, with different gifts and skills, with many faults and flaws. Jesus knew when he called them by name what those gifts and failings were and he still wanted them for service. They were part of his team. All had their own role to play; all had different ways in which they supported Jesus in his ministry. Being called to care today is no different. You are called into a team of people all with different roles and responsibilities. This is not a solo ministry. You will be sent, even if you do not realize it, a team of people to hold you, love you, listen to you, reflect with you, advise you, carry your burdens, weep with you and pray for you. You are not expected by anyone or God to do this work alone, so do not try. Find your special resources, identify them and utilize them to the full. Then you will not only be the best you can be but you will also last the distance.

   In this chapter we have looked at how to sustain ourselves in the face of dealing with difficult situations of pastoral care.

We have looked at how to make use of really positive tools to enhance knowledge, to use reflective practice, and the importance of teamwork in your ministry. We have looked at how to use humour to defuse a situation and how when situations become difficult to bear you can leave them at the foot of the cross and be free to continue your ministry without burden.

Key Points

- Take as many opportunities as you can to complete extra training to enhance your professional and personal practice.
- Use reflective practice to help sustain you, using journal writing, supervision and effective team support.
- Use humour appropriately, being aware of the pitfalls if it becomes inappropriate.
- If you are called to pastoral ministry there will be people who want to help you be the best you can be. Let them aid you in whatever ways they can. Jesus' ministry is team ministry.

Resources

1 Blessing of a still-born baby

Call to worship
May the Lord bless you and keep you
May the Lord make his face to shine upon you
And be gracious unto you
May the Lord lift up his countenance upon you
And give you peace. **Amen.**

Prayer for the baby
Lord of all, we thank you for your work in creation, for your love for all you have made, even in death.
Thank you for (*insert name*) and thank you for taking (*him/her*) into your arms of mercy, keeping (*him/her*) safe from harm and surrounding (*him/her*) with your love.
Thank you for your presence in our sorrows
Take our sadness and fill us with your spirit
Bring us peace we pray, through Jesus Christ our Saviour.
Amen.

Prayer for the parents and family
You knew a mother's love
You knew a father's care
Be with these parents in their loss today
For you can understand their anger and distress
Wipe away their tears
Comfort and console them
Because you are not a stranger but one who knows them and loves them. **Amen.**

Blessing
Into the light of the sun, we let you go
Into the dance of the stars, we let you go
To all who have gone before, we let you go
Go safely, go smiling, go dancing home
We love you, we will miss you. **Amen.**

2 Naming of a baby

Call to worship
As we are gathered, bring us peace
Empty our thoughts of all but you
Let us enter into your presence, in humility and respect. **Amen.**

Reading: Mark 10.13–16 (Bringing the children to Jesus)

Question to the parent/s
What name have you given this child?
(*insert name*) I name you before God and your family and
friends, before those who love and care for you, through our
Lord and Saviour Jesus Christ. **Amen.**

Prayers
Lord, protect, guide, nurture and encourage this child in their
lives. Hold their dreams safely in the palm of your hand.
Whisper your love in their ear when they hit the difficulties
that this world may bring them. Be a guiding light through all
their choices and let your love for them be expressed through
those that are encircling them, through this world and the next.
Amen.

We pray for (*insert name*) family and friends. Grant them gifts
of wisdom, patience and kindness as they uphold (*insert name
parent/parents*)'s in their loving and caring as parents. Give
them the strength to support, to say the right thing at the right
time and to never fail in the task ahead of them. **Amen.**

Blessing
May the grace of God be with you
May the grace of God be in you
May the Grace of God bring you peace. **Amen.**

3 Blessing of a couple when one is terminally ill

Call to worship
We have gathered here today to give thanks for the life and love of (*insert names*) and to give the blessing of God upon their relationship, their love and the time they have together. **Amen.**

Reading: Ecclesiastes 3.1–18 (For everything there is a season)
We have heard how for everything there is a season – a time to love, a time to embrace, a time to laugh and a time to dance. Today we celebrate all you have built together and rejoice in this moment with you. Let us hear the promises you are about to make to each other. **Amen.**

Promises
A   I promise to always love you with all my heart. I promise to trust you, to honour your wishes and to speak for you when you need me to.
    Whatever comes, I promise to be here for you. I will never let the love we have shared be forgotten.
B   I promise to love you with all my heart. I promise to be honest with you and tell you what I need when I need it. I promise to trust you with my life, my love and my wishes.

Blessing of the symbols
May the Lord bless these symbols of love and trust, that they will be a sign that love was here and shared together.

Exchange of symbols
(*insert names*) you have given promises to each other. May the Lord bless you in the love that you have shown and the promises you have exchanged.
Throughout all the seasons there are times of happiness and times of sadness. Today is a day of celebration. We pray for (*insert names*), for their life together for as long as they have; may it be filled with grace and joy.
We pray for the family and friends of (*insert names*). Give them strength and courage to uphold them in their joys as well as their trials. Now let us say together the Lord's Prayer.

The Lord's Prayer

Blessing
Go out into the world to sing and to dance for as long as the music plays, knowing that God sings and dances with you.
Amen.

4 Blessing of a room

Call to worship
Almighty God, we come before you in this place.
As we bow before you, we ask you to come into our presence
bringing peace and protection.

Reading: Psalm 121 (The assurance of God's protection)

Protection and cleansing (during the liturgy flick water onto the four walls)
From the corners of the world, north, south, east and west, we
ask for your peace and protection to descend upon this place.
To cleanse it of anything that hides in the shadows. Bring peace
and comfort to all who dwell here. **Amen.**
Nothing can separate us in life or in death in this world or the
next from the love and protection of God. Let us be reassured
that the presence and protection of God is eternal and everlasting.

Blessing
May the peace of God be with you
May the peace of God be upon you
May the peace of God surround you for all eternity. **Amen.**

5 Prayers before someone dies

Call to worship
In the grace of God, Father, Son and Holy Spirit. **Amen.**

Lord's Prayer

Reading: John 14.1–3, 27 (Peace I leave with you)

Prayers
Faithful God, strong mighty deliverer, who gave your people a rainbow as a sign to remind us of your presence in our lives when the storms of life come lashing down on us. We give you back your child (*insert name*). Hold (*him/her*) safe in your hands, encircle (*him/her*) with your love and holiness. Free (*him/her*) of the pain and suffering that this life has burdened (*him/her*) with.
Like angel wings may the spirit accompany you through the gates of heaven, there to wait without pain and suffering until we will meet again.

Prayers for the family
1 We pray for (*insert name*)'s family and friends as (*he/she*) prepares to let go. Let them not look back with sadness, but forward carrying good, happy memories with them, each and every day, safe in the knowledge that they will be reunited again one day. Until then, let them be at peace. **Amen.**

2 Compassionate, caring God, heal those who are hurting. Be a presence here as long as you are needed, a guiding light for the lost, a rock for those who are faltering. Encircle those who need you most. **Amen.**

3 We cannot hope to understand all that this world shows us. Help us not to get lost asking unanswerable questions, rather let us rest in your presence, safe in the knowledge that your hand is upon us even though we cannot see the way ahead. **Amen.**

Blessing
May the grace of God rest in your heart. May the peace of God give you comfort. May the love of God sustain you through the coming days. **Amen.**

6 Prayers before surgery

Call to worship
Lord, we come into your presence in humility and awe.

Readings:
Mark 4.35–41 (adult)
Mark 9.13–16 (child)

Prayer for the person
Creator God, you made the universe and created all things in your image. Powerful all-loving God, surround (*insert name*) with your love as they go for surgery. Protect them with your mercy and compassion, enfold them into your heart and keep them safe from harm. **Amen.**

Prayer for the clinicians
Be beside the surgeons, nurses and clinicians who will take part in this surgery. May they be guided and strengthened by your power and presence. **Amen.**

Prayer for the family and friends
Be with all who love (*insert name*). Be with us in our watching and waiting. Let the time be filled with hope and assurance. Give them strength to face the challenges this operation will bring. Renew and strengthen them ready for the journey ahead. Be strong for them when they are weak. Carry them when they stumble. Hold them when they are frightened. Understand them when they are angry, for you are a big and loving God. **Amen.**